15

Letter to an Unknown Soldier

Letter to an Unknown Soldier

A New Kind of War Memorial

Edited by
Neil Bartlett and Kate Pullinger

**WILLIAM
COLLINS**

William Collins
An imprint of HarperCollins*Publishers*
77–85 Fulham Palace Road,
Hammersmith, London W6 8JB

WilliamCollinsBooks.com

First published in Great Britain by William Collins in 2014

1

Neil Bartlett and Kate Pullinger assert the moral right
to be identified as the editors of this work

A catalogue record for this book
is available from the British Library

ISBN: 978-0-00-811684-2

Printed and bound in Great Britain by Clays Ltd, St Ives plc

Supported using public funding by

14-18-NOW
WW1 CENTENARY ART COMMISSIONS   **LOTTERY FUNDED**

Letter to an Unknown Soldier was produced in association with
Free Word and commissioned by 14-18 NOW, WW1 Centenary
Art Commissions, supported by the National Lottery through
Arts Council England and the Heritage Lottery Fund

MIX
Paper from
responsible sources
FSC
www.fsc.org   **FSC® C007454**

Find out more about HarperCollins and the environment at
www.harpercollins.co.uk/green

Dear soldier …

Contents

Contents

Our inspiration couldn't have been simpler.

On Platform One of Paddington Station in London a famous First World War memorial by Charles Sargeant Jagger features a life-size bronze statue of an unknown soldier in full trench uniform. He is reading a letter; no one knows who his letter is from, or what message it contains. In the weeks leading up to the hundredth anniversary of Britain joining the war – in a year crowded with official remembrance and ceremony – we invited everyone in the country to pause, take a moment or two, and write that letter.

People responded in their thousands. Some wrote physical letters and posted them to the soldier at Paddington Station; the vast majority posted their letters online to a specially created website. In the thirty-seven days between the 28th of June 2014 (the centenary of the Sarajevo assassinations) and the 4th of August (the centenary of the declaration of war), the soldier received over twenty-one thousand letters. They came from across the country and around the world, and from everyone; from railway workers, writers, schoolchildren, serving soldiers, prisoners, nurses, pensioners – and the British Prime Minister.

The inspiration behind the project may have been simple, but as you will see as soon as you start to read the letters that we have chosen from those thousands for this anthology, people found responding to our invitation far from straightforward. The obvious question of 'What shall I say?' quickly splintered into many more. How can I write if I am not a writer? How can I talk about something as big as war? How should I address a dead person? Do I have to travel back in time and imagine I am writing my letter in 1914, or should I write from now? Am I writing to one man – to a particular named individual from my own family history perhaps – or to all the army of the dead? Is the soldier white, or is he black? Is he British, or Canadian, or Indian, or from the Isle of Lewis? And so on … The beauty of the idea turned out to be that the archetypal and archaic literary form of a letter entitled people to answer these and many other questions in their own utterly individual ways. A letter is not a text message nor a 'like' on Facebook – in order to write one you have to stop, and think, and feel, and compose not just your letter but yourself. A letter is also not an essay nor a short story. A letter is a page or two long, with a beginning and an end. A letter is private. A letter is everyday. A letter is familiar. A letter is, above all, personal.

All of the letters that the soldier received during the thirty-seven days that the website was open for submissions were published without censorship or alteration or editing. In creating this anthology, we have resisted any temptation to organise our chosen letters by theme or place of origin. A bewildering diversity of voice and form was as characteristic of the soldier's daily postbag as the frequent reiteration of often familiar tropes, images, phrases and sentiments. That's why you'll find the letters we've selected in no obvious order, with a politician's letter next to a schoolchild's, a queer love-letter next to a military salute, a soldier's wife next to a pacifist pensioner.

Letter to an Unknown Soldier was commissioned by 14-18 NOW as part of its five-year cultural programme responding to the centenary of the First World War. The entire archive of letters will remain on the current website until 2018, which means that if you want to read more of them all you have to do is go to www.1418now.org.uk/letter/ and start reading. After 2018, the website – including all 21,439 of the letters – will remain part of the UK Web Archive, provided by the British Library. There it will remain permanently accessible, providing future readers with a vivid snapshot of what people across this country and across the world were thinking and feeling in the weeks leading up to the centenary of the outbreak of the First World War. They give us a glimpse of what it means to remember a war that is no longer within lived experience; what it means to remember what cannot in fact be remembered.

Remembrance is usually conducted in silence. This memorial is made of voices – numerous, various, contradictory, heart-broken, angry, sentimental and true.

Neil Bartlett and Kate Pullinger,
November 2014

Dear Unknown Soldier

Imagine you could read my letter now and see how far the world has come since you were fighting in the war. You may have been Unknown then but not now because you have millions of people writing you letters in which most of them are expressing their feelings for you and saying how much of a good person you are.

   If I could meet you now there would be so many questions I would ask you but for now here are just 3.

1. What was your family like?
2. What did you like to do?
3. Who were you fighting for?

_____

Shane Cook
14, London, Holloway School

Dear Owen

Your mother called today, I wish I'd been out.

Anyway I made her welcome.

She sat in your chair, I don't know if she was trying to make a point.

You were very quick off the mark to sign up with your pals.

Not a thought for me or the kids.

Why didn't you take all the clothes I'd laid out for you?

You've only got one pair of smart trousers.

The heavy thick coat is still where you left it.

Your mother said you'll catch your death, what do I care?

And you've left the back gate off its hinge, well I'm not going to fix it.

Anyway I will send you the back pages of this week's *Gazette Times*.

Mind you by the time you get it the runners and riders have already run.

I saw the postman again today, I hung out the washing, as all the women do, we all watched him pass, then we all went back inside.

God Bless.
Mary

_____

Mary Moran
Sheffield

You don't know me yet, but I have things to tell you. You're about to go back, and I'm sorry to say it's going to be worse than ever this time. You're going to be wounded, I'm afraid. Very badly. But you'll survive. You'll make it home. You have to, you see. Forty years from now you'll become my grandfather.

Not that home will be a bed of roses. Wages will be down, and three men will fight for every job. At times you'll be cold, and at times you'll be hungry. And if you say anything, they'll come at you with truncheons.

And then it will get worse. There are some lean years coming. And I'm sorry, but along the way you'll realise: the war didn't end. It was just a lull. You'll have to do it all again. This time your son will have to go, not you. You don't know him yet, but you will. But don't worry. He'll get back too. He has to. You're my grandfather, remember?

And I'll be born in a different world. There will be jobs for everyone. They'll be building houses. You'll go to the doctor whenever you want. I'll go to school. I'll get free orange juice. You'll get free walking sticks. But most of all we'll get peace. Finally, year after year. I will never go to war, you know. I will never have to. The first time I go to France will be a trip with my school.

So go back now, and play your tiny part in the great drama, and sustain yourself by knowing: it comes out well in the end. I promise.

Lee Child
Writer

Dear Soldier

You are strong and brave. You are going to face unknown terrors because you have been told that you are protecting your home and family by fighting the threat of domination and oppression by a foreign foe.

Your finest emotions of loyalty and courage have been subverted by power-hungry empire builders, both politicians and monarchs.

The same lie has been perpetrated in France, Germany, Austria-Hungary and Russia, and will be spread across the globe.

Consequently brave young men across the world have been led to believe that they are doing the right thing by killing one another.

If you could see into the future you would know that this will happen time and again. Young men, and some women too, will be manipulated by those in power to commit murder for the sake of King and Country/the Fatherland/ the Revolution, or for Jihad.

You don't have any quarrel with those young men who speak different languages and have different religious beliefs.

I am asking you to be even more brave.
TURN BACK.
GO HOME.

Show that you can see through the propaganda and that you are not prepared to kill or die for the greed and selfishness of the ruling class.

Meantime, I wish you well and hope that you return safely, and don't come back like my grandfather, whose mental and physical health were ruined after nearly four years at the front.

With love,
Anna Sandham

_____

Anna Sandham
70, Oxford, Grandmother

The letter I didn't send

Dearest Luke

As I watched you walk away with all the other men, marching off to France, I thought I would die from pain. I wanted to wrench you out of that line, take you home to where you belong and know that you would always be safe, and always be you.

This fighting is not for you. You have never been a violent person, you are the most kind and gentle man I have ever known and this will do violence to your soul. I am so afraid that you will come home with nothing behind your eyes but horror and a heart so bounded by stone and afraid of the worst that can happen to people. You would never let yourself love anyone again, through fear of the horror.

I think I fear the damage to your soul as much as I fear you dying. How terrible it would be to live the rest of your life with nightmares, screaming terror and despair.

May God be with you always,
Mum xxxx

The letter I did send

Dearest Son

How proud I was of you as you marched off to defend our country from the Germans, and how wonderful you looked in your uniform. We are all thinking of you, my dearest son, and of the adventures you will have in France. Maybe you will learn a little of the language and eat some wonderful food.

You will be in my thoughts and prayers every minute of every day, my darling boy. Stay well and come home safe to us.

I love you and may God bless you always,
Mum xxx

_____

Sue Oxley
64, Glastonbury, Mother

For my father, who did fight in a war and who came home damaged in his soul.

There you stand, a monument to so many who never returned. Did you leave home whistling, upbeat and expecting adventure? Were you there at the outset, when people still believed the war was just and would be over in weeks, or months at most? How quickly did you realise you had been sold a lie? I look at you and wonder who you knew – did you serve with pals from home, all in together and watching out for each other, or did you join up far away from those who knew you, because you had something to hide? Did you by chance meet a boy called Cyril from Cornwall, who would have claimed to be eighteen, but who was just a child of sixteen? Did you, like him, leave the safety of your hometown to sign up in London, away from the friendly local recruiters, who knew your age and sent you home to your mother? How many were there like him in your unit? How many of them made it home, like he did? How many went on to have children, like Cyril's daughter, my mother?

You can't tell me, of course, but let me tell you something. We still recruit children today, but we do it openly, seemingly without shame. We have learned nothing from your suffering and sacrifice; recruitment remains a numbers game. Children sign up more willingly, they ask fewer questions, and they get paid less. The ones who join up at sixteen these days often don't have many life chances. They are too young to vote, but apparently old enough to serve. My grandfather Cyril was just a boy when he ran away to fight. What an indictment it is on our society that, one hundred years after he joined up, we have not progressed enough to apply the simple maxim 'Children, Not Soldiers' to our own Armed Forces. I'm glad you can't understand, because I believe that if you knew how little has changed, then you, like me, would feel ashamed.

Demelza Hauser
45, St Albans, Mother

*I sit on the Board of a charity which works to prevent the
recruitment of children into armed forces across the world. My
grandfather's story of running away from home in Cornwall
at sixteen to join up in London is part of our family history.
He died when I was very young, so I never had a chance to
ask him about his experiences in the war. It makes me sad
that a hundred years after my grandfather was a child soldier,
we still recruit children into the Army.*

Somewhere in the world somebody is walking on the place where you fell. Or maybe they are lying on their back, face turned to the sun, picnicking with beer and sandwiches. Do crops grow on your grave? Cows move slowly across it? Does a farmhand bend to pick up a bullet casing and put it in her pocket? Has the minefield been ploughed over or left fallow? Are homes built there? Is there a town where once there were battlefields? Fields where once a town stood? Across five continents, one hundred years before you were sent into battle, and one hundred years since, and before and after, and before and after again, lying between layers of earth, under sand dunes, rocking upon the seabed, buried beneath rubble, incinerated into dust: the bones of the fallen. Almost anywhere in the world, wherever one of the living stands now, a warrior has fallen.

We have forgotten their names: The Unknown Warriors. I wonder, at night when the station is still, do they appear from all directions? Dressed in uniforms of every kind, camouflage to cotton and followed by others dressed in the clothes of everyday, farmers' overalls and jeans, business suits, high-heeled shoes, djellabas, rubber flip-flops and leather sandals, shorts, tunics and T-shirts, trainers, sports clothes and sun hats. I wonder if one day there will be another statue standing alongside you, to those people who fell beyond the battlefield, who were queuing for bread when the shells struck, or serving dinner to hotel guests at a poolside restaurant when a grenade was thrown, crossing the street when they were sighted through the crosshairs of a sniper's rifle, sitting in front of their office computer when the first plane struck, shopping in a mall when armed gunmen burst in, walking to the fields when they trod on a mine, buying fruit in the bazaar when the suicide bomber passed by.

Would you even recognise this new kind of warfare? As you board your train to France and the trenches, did you ever imagine it would come to this? Will there come a time when we will commemorate them, lest we forget: a statue, a tomb for them too, uncounted, countless? The Unknown Civilians.

Aminatta Forna
London, Writer

Grandad No 397117

To a unknown soldier,
You may be a friend of my Grandad James Thompson of the East Yorks Hull Batt I have learnt more about you and my Grandad than my dad ever knew as nobody spoke about the war. I am so proud of you and grandad and all the soldier who fought for us. He my Grandad volunteered 4/11/1914 Died 5/10/1918 in Abancourt Hospital France. he was wounded twice patched up sent back to the front in the labour force I hope you fared better than Grandad you and he must have seen scenes which no human beings should be subjected too. I salute you and all brave men, you are all my heros. Mrs J Bilton xx

---

June Bilton
78, Hull, Dove House, Outdoor Lady

Stay safe. Get back. Bring as many back with you as you can manage. Nothing else matters.

_____

Sean
25, USA, US Army, Infantry

For Nathan. I'm sorry I wasn't there, dude. Things might have gone differently.

Hello Tommy

I never knew you, but my Grandfather, Fred, joined up, like
you. He'd been a miner and worked at the pithead at
Senghenydd – leaving just before 440 died in the explosion
on 14 October 1913. He'd left the colliery to go and work in
Dundee, where he also joined the Royal Naval Volunteer
Reserve, before emigrating to New Zealand in 1911.

Three years later, war broke out in Europe and after
working as a gold-digger and miner in New Zealand, Fred
joined the Australian and New Zealand Army Corps
(ANZACs) as a field artillery driver. This involved driving a
team of horses pulling a gun carriage into the field of battle.
A few days after joining up there was an explosion on 12
September 1914, at the Ralph Mine in Huntly, where he had
been working, claiming the lives of 43 men. He must have
sensed then that he had some form of charmed life.

Fred served at Gallipoli and at the Somme, where he was
injured and hospitalised. Like so many others he never
spoke of it afterwards. A million soldiers died or were
wounded during the Battle of the Somme, and 100,000 died
at Gallipoli, so it's incredible that Fred survived both
campaigns, albeit with injuries.

After being evacuated to England on medical grounds,
Fred was visited in hospital by Sarah Jones, who was raised
by his half-sister after her own mother died. They fell in love
and wanted to marry, but Fred was forced to New Zealand
before he could be officially discharged by the ANZACs.
Before he returned to the UK he worked for the Wellington
City fire department.

Fred made it home to Britain safely and married Sarah in
1919. They settled in West Chislehurst, a suburb of south-
east London, and had six children, the youngest being my
father. Never one to shy away from danger, Fred joined the

London Fire Brigade and received a bronze medal in recognition of his 'long and zealous service'. Fred served during the Blitz of the Second World War and must have faced considerable danger most nights. He suffered a number of shrapnel wounds while fighting fires during the war.

In 1944, Fred was discharged from the fire service due to injuries, but he continued to work in the theatres of London's West End as a fireman – responsible for lowering and raising the curtain during each performance.

Fred died in 1967 when I was nine and I wish I'd had the opportunity to talk through his life with him. As I write this, Frederick and Sarah's legacy is six children, 16 grandchildren and 45 great-grandchildren – 67 and counting. History has come full circle now that three of his 2 x great-grandchildren have been born in New Zealand.

So although I never knew you Tommy, I knew one like you and you and all your companions, whether they died or survived are remembered. Thank you.

Barry Rees

—————

Barry Rees
56, Haverfordwest, Grandson

To let Tommy know my Grandfather's story.

I remember the day you went to war. The cockerel was crowing all day, setting the hens to fuss. I had to calm them, Mam shaking her head, saying we'll never get them to sit.

I could tell how far down the lane you'd got. I heard you go by Rose's dogs and then the crows lifted up out of Kings Copse and I thought it was you.

One of Rose's dogs got loose last week. I could hear shouting from up the lane and then one of his collies tore into our yard and flew straight into Jenny. She squawked when he hit her. All the cluck and loveliness come out of her at once. He looked at me then, just to check I understood the rules, then he grabbed her up and set off across Pike's Field.

That evening Rose came round with the dog on a short rope and said we should see it killed. He pushed the dog down onto the lane with his boot on its neck and pulled the rope tight until it couldn't breathe. I could hear Rose grunting as he pulled the rope tighter and the dog started whining through his nose and his eyes fairly popping out. When it was done Rose asked if we wanted the dog's body. Mam said, no, thanking you, Mr Rose, but we'd be happy to take one of your chickens to replace the one we lost.

I don't like Rose. I wish he'd taken the King's Shilling instead of you, and then I got to wondering, if you offered the King his shilling back do you think he'd let you come home sooner?

———————

Martin Daws
Bangor, Poet

Hello Soldier …

Are you coming, going or a little lost? I can't tell.
You look so sad, are you? I can't tell.
You look lonely, so lonely, are you? I can't tell.
You look worn out, exhausted, are you? I can't tell.
Nothing left or more to give? I can't tell.
You look scared, bewildered, are you? I can't tell.
Stiff upper lip or stifling the dread? I can't tell.
Steadfast and proud or reservedly petrified? I can't tell.
A true believer, or believer in fate? I can't tell.
Here's what I CAN tell you … past, present and future.
'Whatever it is, you wear it well, you did us proud, my boy,
    my son, my soldier.'

Love A Stranger xx

Lisa Turrell
43, Solihull, Raisemore, Marketeer

*We work alongside two military charities: Veterans at Ease
and Desert Rats Memorial Association. Both work tirelessly to
support ex-military personnel, recognising the efforts of our
unsung heroes, remembering them with pride.*

Dear Father,

I feel sad because I miss you. Are you okay?

I hope that you don't get hurt.

I miss you reading stories at bedtime and I feel lonely.

Do you feel scared?

I hope you win the war.

I want you to write back please.

Love from Thomas

Thomas Frith
9, Cheshire, Charles Darwin Primary School

With most of us asking the same questions,
among them: did you receive this letter today
or weeks or even months ago and produce it
now to refresh your memory of what it says;
is it a love letter, a letter from home, or lines
from a friend you are happy to know is alive;
who knitted that scarf untied round your neck,
the only piece of non-regulation kit and a clue;
is that a smile on your face or is it just the way
your mouth curves when it is settled in repose;
is it possible you never in fact received the letter
but composed it and now are reading it through
one last time before dropping it in the postbag;
if so, is it a love letter, a letter from home, or lines
to a friend who will be happy to know you alive;
yes with most of us asking these same questions
we forget to think this might not be a letter at all
but a list of questions you have prepared for us,
among them: what makes it possible to end now
our conjectures and leave perfectly free and easy,
heading into town or out to Oxford and the West,
with it making no difference to anything apparently
whether we notice you watching us or fail to notice.

———————————

Andrew Motion
London, Poet

I am the lady in charge of odd parcels, blurry writing, the not-quite-right addresses. I am the investigator, the letter opener, the get-things-running-smoothly woman. I wear a loose uniform and heels that dig in when I walk. I have auburn, curly hair. My mother called me 'homely' once. There are seven drawers in my desk, three down the sides and one across the middle. The bottom right is devoted to you.

There is something thrilling about the tearing of envelopes not meant for your hands. A quick scan – and quick it is, I promise you. I don't want to pry down the words to find addresses, names, ranks, platoons. The clues are threaded together and the letter moves on, or plunges into the bin beside me. Something always feels wrong about binning those, though.

When I found the first letter addressed to 'the girls at home depot' I laughed. Of all the people you could write to, you write to us. I read it out loud on a break, you were so flirty then. Charming and witty like a poet, our warrior poet out on the lines. And punctual too, we looked forward to loopy handwriting on a Wednesday morning. Then you began to change.

Our happy bard grew sad. The letters became too painful to read out, so I locked them in my drawer and left them for days. Something was private about your suffering. After a while I stopped opening the letters.

The letters have stopped. I should have realised sooner, I know. It must be cruel of me, this shameless word-reader, to have left your letters lonely for so long. I resolved myself to burning them in secret, freeing my heart of the burden that is you, my dear tommy. But first, I needed to read.

Sneaking out of the workplace was a cause of some terror for me. I am the girl who is punctual, polite, the early-arrival-who-opens-the-windows. I am not the girl who sneaks out the back door, past the ladies smoking ration cigarettes and to the relative safety of a book store.

I think you must have died. How could you do that to me, without sending so much as a name to call you by? No face to match the words, no frame to fill the hole your letters have left me. My tall soldier, small soldier, blond soldier, brunette soldier. My lost soldier, my found soldier, my brave soldier, my letter-composing coward. I know everything about you, yet I know nothing. How can you mourn someone you cannot prove existed or died? Yet I do, I do.

I am the daughter who aches, who pried, who longs. I am the sister who animates you, runs with you, fights with you and buries you. I am the one who laughs, and cries, and curls up into a ball at the thought of you. I am the one who misses you.

Come to home depot, my silent soldier. I'll be waiting.

Freya Finch Atter
17, Holsworthy, Exeter College Creative Writing Group, Student

I'm assuming I have family that died in the war, but I don't know any of them by name. My grandad lived through the Second World War, but he was kept at home to farm. So when I started writing the letter I didn't have any personal link to build on. Instead I wondered 'What would happen to a letter sent to a false address?' My ideas stemmed from there, until I found my soldier and his woman from the home depot.

Dear Sir,

You are one soldier but you stand for millions. For the millions of young British men who have fought to defend our freedoms and for the millions of us left behind who will be forever in debt to the extraordinary service and sacrifice of your generation.

When you left our shores you did so with hope and purpose. Posing proudly in your uniform, you had a sense of mission and perhaps even of adventure. You knew that you were volunteering to help your country fight a just cause. You did so eagerly, with honour and with the expectation that you might well be home by Christmas.

Today as you read this letter you know, better than we can ever imagine, the monumental horror and suffering of this War.

After what you have seen no-one would blame you for asking why. No-one would criticise you for feeling angry, sad or afraid. Barely any family in our country has escaped unaffected. So many friends have been lost; so many loved ones snatched away from us in their prime. You yourself know you will face further grave danger in the weeks and months ahead.

But be in no doubt; however dark this time of War – our world would have been far darker if you had declined the call to act. Without your service, our security, our values, our very way of life would have been lost.

Know too, that from your toil and sacrifice there will in time be a better world. It will not happen immediately. There will be yet more unthinkable horrors along the way. But one hundred years from now your grandchildren and great-grandchildren will enjoy a peace in Europe and a quality of life that is almost unimaginable.

Historians too will trace back some of the world's greatest advances to your time. From the development of medicine that can heal wounds and sickness to the emancipation of women and the advance of civil rights for ethnic minorities.

Your bravery and selfless determination will never be forgotten. Your name – and the names of your fellow servicemen – will be celebrated on memorials in villages, schools, churches and universities across the land. Plays and poetry will honour you. Painting and monuments will depict you. Ceremonies will be inspired by you. Thousands will write about you, many will even write to you a hundred years from now.

So as you go from here, know that you are in our hearts. Your service will forever be part of our national consciousness. We are humbled by what you have given for us and we will never forget you.

Yours sincerely,
David Cameron

_____

David Cameron
London, Prime Minister

Meadow Community College Marydene Drive Evington Leicester LE5 6HP

Dear Ahmed, My brother

I have been missing you so much. I cannot explain how I am feeling in words. Everytime I walk past your room I am reminded of you and what you could be doing in the trenches. It is no fun without you being here. The weather is very hot here as it always is. Do you remember when we use to play cricket with Gather? Father has been getting better lately and he isn't so depressed about not being able to join the army because of his age. Father has started to help around the house a lot more. He was also wondering how uncle is doing, and if you are still with him. You being gone has had a huge effect on our family. Everybody depends on me a lot more to do the jobs you use to do. You aren't fighting on the front lines are you? Because it's your birthday soon, mother doesn't want to do anything to celebrate it, I think it is too painful for mother to think of you. How is it to fight along side those British soldier? Have you made any friends? I can't remember what you told me about the war. It feels like ten years ago even though it was about 13 months ago. Can you promise to play a game of cricket with me, when you return? We are all missing you so dearly and hope you will return someday, and we will never lose hope you will return. To our village in Pakistan in Karachi.

All the best

Your loving brother, Hassan

24

——————————

Muhammad Hassan Anwar
15, Leicester, Judgemeadow Community College

My English teacher inspired me to write my letter. I would like to dedicate my letter to the soldiers who came from foreign countries to help the soldiers fight.

Dear Unknown Soldier

That is what you are – unknown, unknowable. You are a sign, a symbol: a simulacrum in a shadowy world of simulacra.

There is a gap between what you really are and what you represent, a gap between the fire and the wall, where we stand, transfixed by the shadows in front of us.

Please mind the gap
– the gap between writing this letter and taking real action to rid the world of suffering.

Please mind the gap
– the gap between my sofa and the images of Palestinian slaughter on my television.

Please mind the gap
– the gap between this country and others that don't have commissioned art memorial projects.

Please mind the gap
– the gap between now and then that allows us to remember.

And remembering is important. But I hope, for your sake and the millions like you, that remembering is not all we do.

Yours truly,
An Unknown Soul

Anonymous
West Calder

Dear Soldier,

Standing at your feet, looking up at you, my cousin Susan and I wonder if we ever noticed you before. It's odd, looking with clear blue, fresh eyes at you, recalling our childish days when we struggled by with our suitcases – her miserable and back to boarding school, me happy and off to endless Cornish seaside holidays. Living our separate lives, blonde-haired, blood-tied.

We and our children are part of the line that you saved through your bravery and care, at a time when so many other lines were broken. Is it possible that it was you, on that day, somewhere in France and in a foreign field, in all that noise and terror (when surely the only thing to do was save your own soul), you found Harry Black? Was it you who dragged him up out of the trench that had so nearly claimed his life? He took one, bought one, his comrades had all copped one. Harry, the last man left alive and for three days, barely so, lay waiting to be taken up the line and home to a life-changing but nonetheless dignified life?

Standing at your feet I resolve to write this letter to you, because you need to understand what you did that day. We are the line that will go on to prove you right. There was a world worth fighting for, a line to walk, a line to make and a line to hold.

Love,
Vikki

——————————

Vikki Heywood CBE
Chairman 14-18 NOW

Dear Grandfather,

You met me once, my father said; it was after both Wars, and I was your only grandchild: a babe in arms. Dad said he was afraid to let you see me. Your wife had killed herself the day my Dad was demobbed, though he always suspected you might have murdered her. I think he was afraid you would do something to me, too.

To everyone else, you were a hero – a soldier who came through the Great War without a scratch, an officer and a gentleman. You were pointed out in the street of the small town you came to live, with pride and respect. For King and Country you said, unyielding as your waxed moustache. But to your family, you were the tyrant who took to beating your wife and sons when drunk, and let's be honest, you were drunk most of the time. Once, my father and his brother ran away but it was cold and they had no money, and after three days of hunger they came back, to more beatings. Your speciality was whipping my Dad, then locking him up in a cupboard, because although he was the younger he was the brave one, the one who tried to defend his mother and brother. You weren't the sort of hero who respected courage, or who rescued others at Ypres or Passchendaele. One of your medals was for taking out a nest of machine gunners, one by one. You were a killer, a bully, a dead shot, who had found his natural element in war.

All his life, my father suffered from his own anger, and from trying to understand you; he hated violence and injustice because he had experienced so much of yours. Was it shell shock that made you behave as you did, or your own nature? Was it your own upbringing? Dad said you loved the military life, had been bred for it, brought up to it and expected your sons to follow you into the Army when the next War came along. They joined the Navy and the RAF instead. They spent their whole lives trying not to turn into you, Grandfather, and my father never hit us, or our mother, not once, even when rage and booze boiled through his veins like poison. But Dad would always stop himself. That was his own War – not the one in which he was blown up, shipwrecked and made deaf in one ear. It was the War with you, Grandfather.

Did you have any feelings, or did anger and alcohol consume them all? Was it a form of shell shock, to turn your family into the enemy, long after the War was over? I never knew you, and I never knew my grandmother. She was the loveliest woman, gentle and kind, my father said; an innocent. You would have loved her, and she you. He would weep, remembering, right into his own old age, but he never wept for you.

Amanda

Amanda Craig
London, Writer

Our only boy,

I hope this finds you.
I miss you.

We are doing well as can be expected, considering
everything.
We miss you.

How long is it now? A month, a year? One hundred years?
I've lost track …

I asked your father if he thought there would ever be peace.
He said that people have to *want* peace for there to be peace.
I said people need to be able to *see* peace to want peace. He
said people need to *feel* peace to see peace. You know what
our conversations are like …

I felt peace: When we had you. When you were here.

But since you've been gone – (one hundred years) – I can't
feel it anymore.
And I fear I won't again, until you come back. And stay this
time.

Your room is still empty.
So I have no peace.
So I am no help at all.

Come back to us.
I want to see peace, again.

Your father sends his love.
And I, mine.

Your only Mum

———————————

Stephen Pelton
50, London, Choreographer

Things you do not know:

When you leave, you will leave a child, growing. When night falls on the day you die, your officer will write two letters to two families, yours and his own. He will say to his mother that he has never had to write a letter like that. He has never knowingly lied before. He helped three of his men to bury what was left. He will ask does his mother think, under the circumstances, he did the right thing when he said 'it was quick'?

Your wife and your mother will weep together in the kitchen, over a pot of tea. Your wife will smile through her tears and say, 'At least, it was quick.' Your mother will shake her head and reach for your wife's hand.

Your child, a girl, will be born early, on a hot June night, to the sound of the first bombs to fall on London from a fixed-wing aircraft. Those bombs will hit the school in Upper North Street, and kill eighteen children, mostly between the ages of four and six years old.

You will be moved with infinite care and laid between men you never knew. Your wife and mother choose the words 'Only son and beloved husband' for your headstone. They mean to come and visit your grave when they can save the money. They never do.

Your daughter's husband will be called up to fight in another war. He will leave her, pregnant with her second child, at home with your wife and mother. He will have reinforced the kitchen table with metal sheeting from the works, and they are used to sleeping underneath on a single mattress from the spare bed. Your eldest grandson, a boy of three, lies awake, listening to bombs falling on the streets. He loses his best friend.

Before their own house is hit, killing your wife and mother, your daughter and son are sent away to a farm in Wales. They never go back.

Your son-in-law will be killed at Cassino. Your daughter will not marry again. She helps out at your grandson's school, then trains to become a teacher.

Your grandson becomes a teacher too, lecturing in sociology at Cardiff University, and he marries one of his students. They are pacifists. They do not approve of the wearing of red poppies on Remembrance Sunday but when their son, your great-grandson, comes home from his school, aged five, with a poppy, they let him pin it to the wall chart – but only after an argument.

Your great-grandson will find your photograph in a drawer, and will ask who you are. He is the first person to visit your grave, over eighty years after your death. He will become a military historian, and battlefield guide, keeping your memory alive and the memory of all those who fell with you. You don't know this, but you'd be proud of him.

———————

Vanessa Gebbie
Lewes, Writer

Soldier, acknowledge our salute. I know you will. You'll slam that foot down, like a dog pissing on a tree, this is your ground; you won't move. And as you raise that hand with the same conviction upon which you slam it against your enemies, we will know that you are resolute.

But I want to see into your eyes. I want to see if your convictions are betrayed by your thoughts. Because I worry that we have made you a caricature: the depth of a person is marked by the contradictions within them. I worry that it is too easy to portray you as the valiant hero, the resolute patriot, the loving father. There has to be more to you. And though you were equal to your deeds when you did them, I wonder if you could endure this image after. You cannot be defined by your actions, and if these actions are what we remember, then we do not know you.

Soldier, don't stand for this misrepresentation: leave. Rip through the foundations that hold you down, tear open the tomb that entrenches you. As the material flakes away, we will be reminded of you shaking in the trenches, cold and wet, laden with the burden of self-preservation. But you overcame that burden – how else would you have ended up here?

Overcome another: and as you rise above the material we once thought you were, you give us hope. Because when life kicks me in the teeth, I need to know that I can rise above it. So be the man that meets triumph and disaster and treats them as impostors. Be more than what happened to you; teach us that we are more than what has happened to us. And when our values are strewn into the stream of life, leave us to fish out some new ones.

Soldier, look down. Let us know what you see; because I see the same things differently all the time. And it's really hard to be grounded when you can't find the spot you were standing in yesterday. This river keeps flowing and most of our dads never taught us to fish. So show us where to go.

I think you do that. Your statue was never meant to represent one thing, one position, one person. You stand as a springboard for each of us, to our own little spot. That might be to a conversation with an old relative, or an exploration into our own convictions, or an emblem of a broader notion.

Regardless, you stand resolute. Your stance is firm. Your posture is sure.

Your eyes: a mirror into ourselves.

Sean Spain
22, Bath, Bath Spa University, Student

I have been influenced by Friedrich Nietzsche's concept of the Overman & by Rudyard Kipling's poem 'If –'.

Dear Jack

I know we're not on speaking terms but I've been thinking what if you die.

I've been finding it hard to forgive you and it's worse because I'm the only one who thinks you've done anything wrong. Your family and mine certainly don't.

It was hard to bear the white feathers and specially getting one from Ellen. Don't flap your hand at me, I know you like her. (So do I of course, but you're the hero now.) You'll still say it wasn't the feathers, you just saw the light.

Maybe you're right. Maybe it is sometimes not wrong to kill people. Maybe this war is a glorious exception and

No, I can't think that or only for a short time about four o' clock in the morning. I hope in a way you're still as determined as the day you got on the train and don't have doubts at night to suffer as well as all the other things there. When it's over we can argue about it in the pub.

I keep wanting to say how could you? how could you leave me? and trying to stop myself.

I want you to regret it bitterly. I'm sorry.

Will I send this? It helps writing it anyway. If I go to prison they might not let me write to you so I will send it. I expect your mother will send socks and chocolate. (Ellen too?) So just this from your friend still

Edward

_____

Caryl Churchill
London, Playwright

The power of Love

Dear unknown Soldier

Love. Through all the war and suffering, love still prevailed over all else. People fought for their families, why? Love, that's why. Love is more than chemicals and hormones to those fighting; Love is, was and will always be a motivation. People die for love. That is why this unknown Soldier is a beacon of love; he died for his country, home and all those close to him because he loved them.

Love is the strongest force ever.

don't forget to love

Love prevails.

Never forget to love; this Soldier never did.

Georgina Rees
15, Shrewsbury, Meole Brace School

Love of my friends and family.

Dear Tom

I hope you don't mind if I call you Tom. But I seem to have got to know you quite well over the years. You see I was a policeman at Paddington Station for a number of years and I walked past you almost on a daily basis and each time I spared you a thought and what a great man you were having given your life for King and Country.

You will also be proud to know that Royalty has been rubbing shoulders with you for decades. Members of the Royal Family and indeed other famous people often boarded their train from platform one, from where you now stand. My colleagues and I spent many hours keeping the Royal Train safe and escorting the various dignitaries, but you've probably been watching all these comings and goings for years.

You've probably also watched the unsavoury things in life that occurred right under your nose, the vagabonds and ruffians who frequented the station to commit crimes. Nothing much has changed since you were a boy.

My grandad served in the Great War and whilst he spoke little of his experiences fighting abroad, I did find out years later some of what he went through. Having served in the Boer War in South Africa he went off to fight again in 1915 in the Gallipoli Campaign. Although he was seriously injured fighting overseas he fortunately survived to be repatriated to the UK and to live to a good age.

So Tom I can imagine what you may have gone through. But unfortunately you didn't have the chance to see your grandson, like my grandfather did. So I'd just like to say to you, thank you for sacrificing your life for my generation to be able to live in peace. I and very many more people will always be eternally grateful to you and the many millions of your comrades who gave up so much.

Tom, as I am now retired, I may not be passing you at Paddington Station very often these days, but I will never ever forget you as a great bloke and a very brave soldier.

Thank you Tom and God Bless You.

—————————

John Owen
68, Grantham, British Transport Police History Group, Retired

Letter from the Unknown Soldier

I am not able to write adequately about the people and the country of France. Whatever one sees is different from our Punjab villages. They have here pleasant gardens, houses made from bricks, roads and carriages. The soil is beautiful, corn or roses would grow quickly if planted.

We are treated well and given blankets and food, even a scarf which I am now wearing to help me fight the cold weather. The bread is like a baton which is hard on the outside and soft in the middle, it is acceptable. We are eating of the salt of the King and loyalty becomes us.

Yet all around us are scenes from the wars in the Mahabharata and the Ramayana. So I take heart from your words, that Time is ruled by God, that my breath is in God's will. But how I grieve for you, for all at home, that the plague is spreading. You are ever before my eyes. What more can I say.

Letter to the Unknown Soldier

How strange to receive your letter written not in Punjabi but in English. And here I am writing in foreign. Our reader and writer is a kind Brahmin in town who charges little. I have to tell you, it is true, as you must have heard from the other soldiers, the plague has come like a scythe to corn and is spreading from village to village for its grim crop! We remain safe and have turned to the snake priest who sprinkles the houses with fire to ward off evil; we make daily puja at his shrine. Dear husband, remember God is everywhere, his will is in the drinking water which becomes holy when you drink it with a prayer.

The rains have come so do not worry for the crops. The cow is giving milk and we have a good store of corn. I hope you are being treated well, that you are given our food and that foreign is green with mountain water as we have it here. The name of the German is breathed like that of the demon Harankash. There are rumours he is coming to Punjab but we know the King will send him packing.

How soon married, how soon we have been parted. I must not forget your smile and your always kind words. My husband, fight like a man and come home a hero with the shadow of God in your stride. What more can I say.

Daljit Nagra
Harrow, Writer

Dear Boy

I can't stop thinking about you as you head off for the great adventure in France. You look very marvellous in your uniform: it is funny how a uniform turns a boy into a man so quickly.

I just wanted to say goodbye properly before you leave on the train, to remind you that even though you are excited now, things will change; and sometimes you will feel very wretched and frightened and not bright and happy as you were when the train pulled out of the station and you were all singing and waving your caps.

Always remember that you must take care of your friends and mates who will be having a rough time as well: try to keep your spirits up, even when it looks darker than hell. I don't know how sorely you will be tested but at all times be as brave and kind as can be. I have put some cough lozenges in your kitbag and a vest for when it is cold. Remember to read, as that will take your mind off the guns. Look out for birds and flowers, as they are the signs that in the end all will be well; and if you meet local people please be polite (Bonjour, merci, au revoir).

Will you write to me? Writing is like an escape, and that is why I am writing this now, as I think that if I saw you I would cry my eyes out at having to say goodbye.

I don't know what will happen, but every day and every moment I will be thinking of you, my Boy.

Come back safely xxxx
Your loving mother

Joanna Lumley
Actor

I wanted to express my gratitude … is what I find myself writing from habit. I'm not sure gratitude is the right word, because I'm not too sure I'm for the war, or any war for that matter.

And I'm not sure whether you're out there by choice or by duty or if the two can ever be intertwined. I could talk about home or ask you what it is like out there, in the mud and the cold and the rain. I could talk about the women down the road sewing as if it will mend everything, or about my widowed neighbour who stares forlornly at the forget-me-nots in her garden and no longer speaks, not even to the milkman. But I don't think these trivialities will put light in your heart and it is light in your heart that might pull you through the struggles that arrive with each new day. So I will tell you a story with the aim of spiriting you away to a gentle place …

After a while all the cold mud grows warmer, and the air hot. Rainforest plants appear, thick and moist and green, and they open to a lake from which steam rises. All around birds of paradise sing.

The butterflies float iridescent in the humidity and the bright tree frogs gaze longingly at the flies. A beautiful person swims there, in the lake, every day, at the foot of a ramshackle jetty which rises from the door of a house made of reeds to the bank. This ethereal being kisses the water as it flows past their nakedness. Time subsides. Reaching the bank, they raise their body glistening from the water, drawing their legs up to their chest. And then their eyes, like other fantastical worlds, invite you to join them, as temptation stretches out across the sand, waiting.

––––––––––––––

Sophie Collard
27, London, Writer

43

Darling

I don't know if you'll ever get this letter but I had to write it anyway.

Sorry for any spelling mistakes. You know I'm writing this quick and urgent as I need to catch the postman, and you know spelling was never my strongest was it, not never in school. But Roddy. I have to tell you, in case – well I can't write it here – but you know what I'm thinking. I have to write so that I can think of you over there, with my words tucked up in your pocket next to your heart.

Of course your wife will write you too, going on about the boys and the socks she's knitting and stuff like that. Everyone else is allowed to write you. Your mum. Jenny, Nanna. Everyone except me. But you know, don't you, things I can't never say? I have to say them. Otherwise my heart is going to crack right open like a walnut shell.

That day you left. The line you was in with the others – you remember me running alongside, and then stopping when I saw Alice. I was trying to tell you. Something I think you've guessed. And whatever happens, whatever – I won't never get over you and I won't never find another man if you don't come back and I don't care what anyone says about war and fighting but what we did was real too wasn't it, what we did matters? It was true and ours, and it's the only thing that matters in this world really isn't it? It's the only thing that lasts, that can save us – Roddy, darling, I have to tell you!

You're a good man Roddy. I know you was scared that night and lonely and you wasn't thinking about Alice and you didn't mean to hurt no one it was just a long time we'd loved each other and not given in to it, wasn't it, all those years in school and that, but for me it wasn't like that at all. It wasn't a mistake, no, and it wasn't the war neither. It was the most special thing I've ever done. It will always be that to me. So Roddy, I won't tell a soul, all right, I promise. I just wanted to write you this letter. I'll raise her or him by myself to be a good person I won't let him go to war neither if he's a boy or maybe I will if it's a good cause, right, like what you're doing. I'll do a good job I know I will – I always wanted to be a mother.

I can bear anything, I'll go away to a home to have my baby, I won't bring a scandal, I'll raise him right – I hope it's a son Roddy, I hope he grows up into a good man like you – I'll bear whatever people want to throw at me.

If only you'll keep safe Roddy. Please, Roddy. Just keep yourself safe and come back.

Your loving Ruby
xx

————————

Jill Dawson
Ely, Writer

I think there were a lot of women who suffered in silence about losses because they weren't recognised as girlfriends, wives or mothers, because their hearts contained secrets. Women who couldn't mourn openly. I think someone I know – now ninety-two – is one such woman. I wanted to write a letter from her.

Dear Unknown Soldier

What a stupid statement. I know exactly who you are. So if I know you, then you cannot be unknown – well not to me anyway.

I never met you. You had gone to fight in that terrible, terrible war many years before I was born, but that doesn't make any difference.

I grew up knowing that you – my great-uncle – had died in Belgium, fighting over some unpronounceable woods, and that you had been 'killed in action', at least that is what the telegram said. A telegram that my grandmother, your sister, took from the ashen-faced telegram boy.

'Killed in action' the telegram said, but what it didn't say was that you had probably been atomised. There was no recognisable trace of you left to bury. No grave for us, your family, to mourn over.

Yes I know your name is on a wall, which is on a panel and which makes up the focus of remembrance that is the Menin Gate, in Ypres.

The Menin Gate – the British Memorial to the Missing – and you are not alone.

Alongside you are the names of 54,338 other poor souls who like you, 'have no known grave'.

I like to think, as I stand below your name, that you are aware of who I am and that I am there on behalf of the rest of your family.

Your family. Did you know that your mother, father and youngest sister Ethel had travelled to Belgium in 1928, as pilgrims on the then 'British Legion Pilgrimage'? They had stood beneath the same panel that I have. Did their tears make you weep?

I've often wondered whether even for the briefest of moments, you could have left your panel and wrapped your arms around them. A family, together again.

Your mother never got over your death. Her grief was absolute. The love your mother had for you and the spectre of grief that had wrapped itself around her, escorted her to the grave.

How cruel is fate? I truly hope that you were aware that your father departed this life on September 29th 1938 – twenty years to the day that you departed. How symbolic was that.

As I write this, I am looking at a photo of you, taken when you were a young man; a young man who seemed full of life and yet who was to have that life cruelly taken from him – and us.

I freely admit that the statue of the unknown soldier doesn't look very much like your photograph, BUT IF I WANT TO BELIEVE THAT IT IS YOU, THEN THAT'S WHAT I'M GOING TO BELIEVE!

Until I write again, I'll leave you with the final line from one verse of the hymn, 'Jesus, Lover Of My Soul':

'Safe into the haven guide; O receive my soul at last.'

God Bless You
Your Great-Nephew

Gareth Scourfield
67, Caerphilly, Royal British Legion and The Western Front Association, Retired

This letter is my chance to write to my great-uncle, who was Killed in Action in September 1918.

Brave soldier, perpetual myth:
The sacrifice slaughtered on
politician altars and citizens
needing a quick idol. 'Look
how much better – look
how much worse –' You,
soldier martyr and Saint
Patriot, named but by your
nation and known but by your
cliché: You journey forth bold
and confident (how else would
you go?), and die a death
cinematically heroic. Fears
dismissed, doubts diminished –
And have I said it yet?
Thank you for dying.
Thank you for dying.
Have you heard about the Xbox?
Thank you for dying.
Thank you for dying.
Take it on assurance, this
is how you wanted it – death
made meaningful in strangers'
memories (and maybe it's
true, maybe we do preserve
you in fleeting thoughts meshed
between 'I'm hungry' and 'Hey,
there's McDonald's'). But
when 'sacrifice' is pandered
beside 'LOL' and 'like' and the next
Big Issue, does the word not
lose its value? Cheap and rendered
meaningless in repetition – And have I
mentioned you must be handsome,

strong, and honourable; what other
kind of soldier is there? And maybe
you are that way, maybe –
You are that soldier's ancestor, the one
who talked the woman and kids trapped
in their house through eight hours of Taliban
shooting, the soldier who would not
let her hang up and face it
alone. But maybe you weren't, maybe –
you are more like those who say
they would shoot any Afghan;
who cares if she's pregnant?
Maybe you swear and drink
and women fight instead of fancy
you. Is it blasphemy to say:
One does not become a hero
simply by having died?
Unknown but claimed by everyone,
you've lost your identity, sir,
it belongs to us, sir, to make
not into a mirror
but a manipulation. You
are mine to say 'noble.' You
are mine to say 'tool.' You
are mine to say 'hero.' You
are mine to say 'waste.' You
have no voice. You
have no memory. You
are mine to make a myth.

Alyssa Hollingsworth
23, Fort Monroe, USA, Bath Spa University, Graduate
Student

Dear Soldier –

I see you there. You are gripping that letter, and you are angry.

We are asked to remember, but it isn't easy. I have no experience of war and what it does to you, even though the troops – the British, the American, the Syrian, the troops in so many countries, in fact – are engaged in war almost continually. The closest I've come to your war is the memorial in Ely Cathedral; my great-uncles, W. A. Low and H. Low, both killed at the western front, are named on it. I didn't know those uncles. My mother, their niece, didn't know them either; they were killed before she was born.

My grandfather – their brother – left England during your war; he married my grandmother, fled the Fenlands and travelled to Canada, beating conscription and thus avoiding their fates. He died before I was born. I look at you on your plinth, soldier, and I think: how can I remember people I never knew? How can we know the unknown soldier?

My family has no artefacts, no touchable, tangible family history. When my mother died and we emptied my parents' house, the only remnant of their parents' generation was a badly made plywood plant-holder that my grandfather, a railway worker, knocked together in the 1950s.

A railway worker, like you. But alive and well in 1918, the year, perhaps, you lost your life; head down, hard at work, making a new family on a big lake in a fertile valley in the westernmost reaches of the new Dominion, far far away from Europe and the dirt and the blood and the horror. Eventually, he built a house for that family to live in. They thrived. My mother married a man who had been to university.

But you, you died on a battlefield. You got more than you bargained for, I imagine, like W. A. and H. You stand there, gripping that letter, and you are angry. You look up, away from the letter, at us, all the people, one hundred years later, and you open your mouth and you roar. You roar at everyone gathered at the cenotaphs and memorials, you shout at everyone with their speeches and their sermons and their poppies and their wreaths, and you fill those minutes of silence. You want us to listen to your message.

But we don't hear you. We drag our suitcases up the platform past you and we look at our phones and we worry about missing the train, and we do not hear what you are saying. And the troops are deployed, and re-deployed, all over the world, again and again.

Kate Pullinger
London, Writer

Tommy reads his orders
And despite his greatcoat,
Feels the cold inside his brain.

How to tell his friends?
There'd been no training for such a job.
That they must go over the top again.

If a friend fell beside him,
What then would he say or do?
Would he stride on as taught
Or stand like a statue waiting for a train?

———————————

Richard Ireson
67, Romford, Pensioner

*My maternal grandfather fought in WW1. Dedicated to all
who fought.*

Dear husband

It feels almost normal now, these letters, our only communication since countless months, or perhaps years? I read and re-read your every word till I have memorised not just the words but even the rise and fall of your lettering; the winding ink trails carved in your strong hand, every bit as sacred to me as the holy Alaknanda and Bhagirathi rivers that carve through and feed our land, just as your words feed my soul.

Do you remember, as children, I would watch you playing with your friends, scrambling over the rocky banks of the Bhagirathi, claiming the land in the name of the Shah? Afterwards, you would come back home with me, and we would swing on the rope swing hanging from the mango tree in the courtyard, where I sit again now, remembering and writing. You talked even then about teaching our children to climb and pick the mangoes.

Who knew then that just days after our marriage, the foreign King would need you to go to strange lands and fight his war? Did he not realise that there were others who needed you more? We who fight our own daily battles, for whom life itself has become war. But who thinks of us? Not this foreign King, not the foreigners whom your blood and sweat defend. Who will remember us, unknown soldiers of an unknown war?

On your sister's birthday last week, we visited the temple of Jwalpa Devi. The pandits there told how Yamaraj, the Lord of Death, stalks the land of Europe. Let the recruiters sing of glories and riches; everywhere there is talk of great suffering, the great destruction of this 'Great War'. And still I ask, as I asked when you were leaving, do those distant foreigners know, or even care, who it is who fights and strives, so they may wage their war? Are even you, who give your all, just another unknown soldier?

You wrote to me that the destructive force of this war matches the Mahabharata itself. You wrote how you despaired that men inflict such horrors on each other, how you yourself have killed those with whom you had no quarrel. Where in this Kurukshetra is Krishna, to guide and protect my Arjun?

But for all that, we are children of Bharati. We both know that we must do our duty, we each must fight our battles ahead. Dharma offers no recognition, no thanks, no reward but itself. Keep reading the Gita I gave you as you left, and find strength in those powerful, divine verses. And remember that the Mother Goddess resides in our every noble act. By Devi Mata's will, and with Her blessings, we will soon once again bathe together in the cool waters of the Bhagirathi, and swing together under our mango tree. Until that day, remain strong my dear husband, and know that I am, always,

Yours completely.

———————

Dr Manish Tayal
37, Salford, We Were There Too, Doctor

Lost somewhere between Europe's heavy personal grief and the shame of proud new nations of their history of foreign rule, lie the stories of 1.3 million Indian soldiers, their lives, and the lives of those they left behind, all but forgotten. War does not just kill soldiers, it destroys whole families, and entire villages.

This letter, from a Garhwal wife to her husband, is dedicated to those countless and unknown soldiers – wives, children, parents, siblings, friends, and of course, the soldiers themselves. May their stories never be forgotten, and today, as war still rages on, may their words echo through the past century to act as a warning and a guide to us all.

'Awayfarers' 54 St Mary's Street Bridgnorth
17th July 2014

Dear Soldier of the Great War,

I have passed by the place of honour where you lie a few times, the first time when I was a boy in short trousers. It was 1951 the year of the Festival of Britain, an event to cheer up the nation after the Second World War. Me and my cousins were very excited; in the late afternoon mother and Aunty Irene took us into Westminister Abbey to calm us down. There we saw your resting place in the nave.

My mother was a strong woman she never did show much emotion but when she read the plaque on the floor that said a British Warrier brought from France was resting below she

Graham Hugh Jones
75, Bridgnorth, The Royal British Legion, Ex-Airman

had a 'funny turn' and had to sit down in the nearest pew. You see she thought she was standing by the grave of her Uncle Edwin. He fought with the King's Shropshire Light Infantry and died on the Somme. At the end of his last leave he called to see her, she was a teenage servant working in a house near the railway station. She never knew that he was buried alongside his comrades near Serre, she always believe that you were her dearly-loved uncle. This was a great comfort to her to believe that he was in a special place, loved and mourned by the nation.

Thank you for helping her to bear the grief.

Graham Jones.

Inspired by a girl called Nell. Dedicated to my father, Gunner Andrew Jones, a veteran of the Great War.

Beloved brother

Enough time has passed now for us to think only one thought: that we will never see you again. The last I heard you were cheerful and funny, as ever.

Remember when I told you that I was going to declare myself a conscientious objector? I saw a look in your eye. 'My brother, a coward?' It nearly killed me. I would give anything to be in your place, a hero respected and at peace – and not just because of the insults, beatings and stones hurled at me from bus conductors, shopkeepers and children in the streets.

Every night Ma and Pa sob as they try to swallow their food. I eat in another room. They cannot look at me. I try not to feel sorry for myself, but I do believe it is wrong to kill. I made my decision. You made yours.

For eternity your image will stand for unquestioning courage. I will die proud of you and ashamed of myself. And that is in spite of me being right.

———————————

Stephen Fry
Actor

Grandfather

My eyes can never see you; I don't know why. Is it because I'm blind? I've always wondered, where have you been? I found myself thinking the obvious, you were in the war. Where I am now feels lonely. Maybe the same with you. The verdant grass has always covered the mud. The salty seawater taught the sand.

Nowadays, it's all films and games. Nothing special. Just simple Boredom. What happens next? Sleeping in bed all day? I would hate that. Everybody seems to think of you as the Unknown Soldier, and yes you were. Nevertheless, I think of you differently. Although you were a soldier, you were my best person of history. The one who would share strange experiences. The one who didn't resist.

It's like hell on earth here, but it was worse for you! I didn't realise how bad it was until I heard about it. You were in hell, not me. You had to run across trenches filled with thousands of gallons of dirty water.

I can feel it. You. Watching above me giving me the subtle signs to the pathway of a great life. I know you're around me everywhere, every time, but I just can't distinguish it. I was always the mud. If only you were the grass. I wish I could see you properly.

From your proud grandson,
Jason

Jason Chua
14, Colchester, Colchester High School

I bet you thought that the fighting was worth it back in 1914. You bravely stormed in, thinking you would be changing the world and making it better for everyone; that you were fighting to protect your country and the people in it. You were fighting for freedom by sacrificing your own life. Did you have any idea that, in the way it always does, history would repeat itself and that a century later more men would be heading into the trenches, mirroring the actions of their brothers, 100 years before?

There will always be discontent. There will always be somebody intent on causing pain and suffering and thousands more, pouring in, trying to plug the evil! Doing their bit. It's 2014 now, and a war has been raging in Afghanistan for twelve years, eight months and three weeks. Constant, ongoing conflict causing utter destruction and pain to civilians and soldiers alike. A refusal to back down has resulted in tens of thousands of men and women being killed. Among those was my friend, 1st Lt Tyler Parten. He had a zest for life, possessing all the traits of a great friend and leader: intelligence, compassion, courage and desire. He saw things through the eyes of a man who held strong in his faith, beliefs and morals. But on September 10, 2009, he was shot in Afghanistan, leaving a mum, a dad, a younger brother and a little sister. He left behind a girl that thought one day she would marry him. It ripped that family apart, right at the seams.

Who did you leave behind? This is a letter to the Unknown Soldier. So many remain nameless and while I'm sure it was not in vain, I do wonder ... what was and is the true cost of war?

———————————

Sarah Spain
30, Beaconsfield

For a missed friend.

my fellow

our last night.
after, watching you on the side of the bed
lacing your boots up
2 hands in quiet motion.
after, walking in mute drizzle to paddington
where to say goodbye.
platform ticket pinched, my thumb to forefinger.
hands are firmly shaken,
you do not blink. we. don't. blink.
after, your train left me on platform 1
and that, my love, was that.
after, you never returned
i will always find you here
on platform 1.

x
dom

Dom Agius
45, Brighton, Photographer

Dear Unknown Soldier

Did you happen to meet John McNaught? We cannae find him. If ye see him will ye pass these words to him from us?

How sad, Johnnie, that you left the beautiful Argyll countryside of Dunoon expecting to return a hero but not returning at all.

You had so much to come back to, so much love and warmth. Aye, ye missed it all, our bonnie John.

Your mum and dad met on the Glasgie ferry. He was the ferrymaster. He stayed alive for many years after you died. Notice that I write 'stayed alive' and not 'lived', for he mourned ye every waking hour. My brave John, to this day your name still greets the tourists landing in Dunoon at Hunter's Quay. You are unknown to those tourists but not to us. And yet we knew you as a young boy really, not a man. Ye didn't have the chance to be a man and do what other men do.

John, if you had lived to return from France to tranquil Dunoon you would have grown up in peace alongside your brother and sister. Unlike them you didn't marry or have children. Unlike them you missed out on the misty Scottish sunsets and sun risings. You missed out on family dinners. We all sat around then and remembered you ... mourned you. Cried for your lost opportunities. Cried for your lost body. Your ma and da were so upset at hearing that your body could not be found and there was no grave upon which they could place flowers. Flowers for their bonnie wee John blown to smithereens a month after landing in France in that war said to be great, but not at all great for us.

RIP Unknown Soldier and thank ye for taking this to our John. For after all he has waited for nigh on 100 years to hear from us.

Amanda Crinson-Loutfi and the Loutfis of England, Syria and Kuwait

———————————

Amanda Loutfi
49, Braintree, Mother

Dear Unknown Soldier

If only I could talk to you rather than writing a letter – but then what would we say if we were face to face? You would surely find me strange – an old woman by your lights, and one who is wearing trousers and doing what you would see as a man's job. Worse, I fear that you would find me obtuse, tactless and insensitive.

I want to ask you so many questions but would you want to answer them? Soldiers in your war – and I suspect that it is true of most – find civilians intensely irritating with their talk of glory and heroism, their unwillingness to accept that war is so often boring, dull and mindless when it is not about killing or being killed. Civilians are full of hate for the enemy. I suspect you are more likely to feel sympathy for those soldiers across No Man's Land. Those poor sods, I can imagine you saying, they're caught up in the same mess.

Let me start with an easy question. Who are you when you are not a soldier? Where do you come from? From remote farms, in the Welsh hills perhaps or in deepest Cornwall? Is the war the first time you have been in a city or seen a big railway terminus like Paddington? Or are you a clerk from a City office, snatched from your comfortable routine of train in, train out, rain and shine? When you go home what is it like? I so wish I could place you. Is it a farmhouse kitchen, a pretty house in the suburbs, or a London flat?

Can we talk about class? Do you have a rich father? A university education? Unlikely I suppose given that the upper classes are such a small section of society. It's more likely that you are from the middle or working classes. They're so many more now. Perhaps you belong to a union. They've been getting quite militant lately, haven't they?

I can't help but be more personal still. You look very young to me. Have you been in love? Oh please tell me that you have. You are reading a letter – let it be one from someone you love and who loves you. I do so hope that you and your loved one – girl or boy, we don't care so much about that these days – have had time to throw yourself into each other's arms. OK – I'll stop there because I suspect that I am making you blush but I have to tell you that it is so *unfair* if you have been swept from the earth without enjoying some of the pleasures of being human.

War isn't fair of course – I scarcely need tell you that – and we rely on the young like you to fight them. Old people do not make good soldiers. The young do because they are full of energy and readier to be brave and reckless. You went off hoping you would come back. Forgive me for being blunt but you haven't. Nor have millions of others.

Whether it was worth it I will leave to others to decide. I just wish we could talk about it all.

Yours affectionately
Margaret

PS I don't want to call you Unknown any more.

———————

Margaret MacMillan
Oxford, Historian

Dear Soldier

I know that you are unknown to me and the people that are living now. Nevertheless, we all feel thankful to all of you that have fought bravely, thinking about your individual family. All of us that are living now are living from the braveness that you all have left us.

If I was there, where you were, I would start to hate humans. I would be scared that I am human. I would want to be a shell in the dark, deep ocean and roll around the sea, peacefully. I would think to myself carefully about what is life. I would try to think positively but I bet I couldn't.

Soldiers died. They died because they disappeared from people's memory. Do people die when they get shot by a gun? No. Do people die when a bomb explodes? No. Do people die when they get poisoned? No. People die, people die when they get forgotten.

Yours in memory.

_____

Oska Read
12, Littleborough, Wardle Academy, Student

Dedicated to people that have been forced to go to war and to my great-grandfather who fought in the First World War.

It's been nearly 100 years, and I'm still amazed at the outstanding effort that you lads went through and sacrifice you all gave. Not just in lives but in what you went through. I have experienced a small amount of what you have been through. Seen my friends killed and wounded but each night was back in my FOB safe behind the wire. You defended not just our shores but our whole way of life, from a bigger evil who wanted to wipe our homes off the face of the earth.

I am so proud to be in the Army, knowing that the history you made set a standard that we will never allow to be lessened. I went to France a few months back, it was heart-breaking seeing how many were killed. Looking at a cemetery and then thinking 'I have six hundred lads in my Regiment, and there are seven hundred lads here.'

I'm sorry we have let you all down. Your war was meant to be 'the war to end all wars' but tyrants carried on doing bad things, that has required the men and women of this great Country to come to the aid and defence of those who want to live free of fear. The mark you have left and the soldiers who still remain on these battlefields will ensure that we will never forget what you have all done for all of us.

Thank you.
You will never be forgotten.

Cpl SM Cleator
ARMD TP, 33 AES
26 ENGR REGT.

Stephen Cleator
35, Salisbury, 26 Engineer Regiment, Tank commander

For all my family who fought and died in WW1.

My dear friend

Thinking of you today as I write this letter makes me realise you have been with me all along.

You were there when I lived as a boy and my school made me wear a uniform and walk every day under an archway on my way to classes. The archway had the names of your comrades from both world wars carved into it: the names of all those who had been murdered in the conflict. And the other side of the archway was the huge statue of the brooding man, the field marshal, who our country honoured for stifling his humanity and sending you to your deaths.

We were made to wear army uniform on Monday afternoons, uniform of the kind they made you wear, and blanco our puttees and polish our buckles and our boots. We were inspected on a parade ground and made to march up and down carrying rifles while sergeants shouted at us.

The rifles came from your war. You had to carry them too; and later we were taught to take them apart and oil them and grease them and then fire them at targets with human faces.

This was done to us for the same reason it was done to you: to make us into what they called men.

And so I associated my hatred and fear of all this with my deep desire not to be a man at all.

Longing to be a woman was something I was so ashamed of because I had been told, like you, that to be like a woman was the worst shame of all.

As I grew older, my dear friend, I learnt of your sufferings and the desperate cruelty of it all and like so many of us came to understand that what we had both been taught about the glory of war was a terrible evil lie.

To think of war as something unnecessary and cruel was

almost impossible when you were alive; but you helped strengthen that thought in us.

And along with that understanding it became more and more possible for me to learn to respect, honour and love the woman in me and to allow her full and open expression in my life.

Which is why now, as a woman, I have come here with all the other travellers to stand at your feet and honour you.

My dear love, you must have felt so helpless.

But there was a power in you that you knew nothing of.

Your death taught us that we do not have to go to war.

That there is another way.

That in honouring compassion, pity and mercy, those so-called women's qualities, we can learn to truly honour the women in us.

And then, as humans, truly understand what it means to be a man.

With love and thanks,
Jo Clifford

———————

Jo Clifford
Edinburgh, Writer

Dear John

You should get this just before you go over the top in what we now call the Battle of the Somme. It's a couple of hours before dawn. You are cold, half asleep, and both terrified and excited.

There's no easy way to tell you this but in three short hours' time you will be dead, one of 19,240 Brits killed on this day. But I hope this letter will bring you some small comfort, some reassurance that you did not die in vain in this, the war to end all wars.

You have a little boy at home, also called John, just a couple of years old. He will grow into a fine young man, he will follow you into the army and he, too, will have a son called John. Your son will be killed in the Arab insurrection in Palestine in 1936. A brave man trying to keep the peace, he will be blown up by a crude homemade bomb.

By now, joining the army is becoming something of a family tradition. Your grandson, John number three, is too young to fight in the next great European conflict but he is old enough to suppress the Mau Mau uprising in Kenya, where he will be speared as he walks back to barracks one night in 1954.

John number four has no far-off colonial adventures. He and his two mates will fail to return from a night patrol in Belfast in 1972. His body is never found.

His son, your great-great-grandson, and my dad, John number five, performs bravely in the first Iraq War, the only one of the family to be awarded a medal. He will die in 1991 while trying to rescue comrades from a burning tank, hit – we believe – by friendly fire.

Last century, your century, like all of the human centuries before it, was disfigured, shaped and transformed by violence. I am sorry to be telling you now, just before your own life ends, that I will not be part of this. I am the first man in our family for over a century not to join the army and yesterday morning I held in my arms my newborn son.

Tomorrow I leave with my camera crew to film the conflict in northern Iraq. I have to show people the horror, not participate in it. Even so, my wife fears I will not return.

I love you, John, and I respect you. I hope your death is quick and painless and I pray that you join all those other Johns in peace. We will all join you in time.

Your great-great-great-grandson
John

_____

Roger Jarman
64, Exeter, Human

From every anonymous wife beater to the President of the United States, we humans seem ridiculously wedded to the notion that the solution to any problem – real or imagined – is violence. A slap, a punch, an IED, a drone. I just wish that we could stop!

Dear all of you

I'm so sorry about summer 2004. On that school trip to the battlefields and memorials of France and Belgium, I couldn't feel a thing. I stood numb at the Menin Gate and wondered what was wrong with me – I was a melodramatic teenager, I could get emotional about what to have for breakfast, so why not this? We'd all been given a booklet to fill with our reflections, and I peppered mine with exclamation marks ('Found the grave of a 17-year-old! The same age as my best friend's brother!') in an attempt to jolt my heart into feeling something, anything. The few uncertain emotions that did rise to the surface – discomfort with the sanitised white of the British cemeteries, a conviction that the German Langemark cemetery held more tragedy in its dark tree-shadowed corners – were quickly contradicted by my classmates. Langemark was too hidden, ashamed of itself, they said; our cemeteries honoured the sacrifice made in a more dignified way. I clammed shut again, retreating into fake exclamation marks and guilty relief when we visited a Belgian chocolate factory instead of a memorial.

Then, two months later, I read Wilfred Owen's 'Dulce et Decorum Est' for the first time. I'd seen the poem before, of course, but the Latin title had made the rest of the words seem hopelessly unrelatable, not even worth bothering with. This time, sitting in an English classroom, every word stabbed into my heart like something I'd never known before. It was the first time poetry had made me feel anything. I wanted to run down the corridors screaming it. I walked the streets of my paper round that evening with Owen's words burning in my brain. I thought of nothing else for days – no, months if I'm being honest. Suddenly I knew what I should have felt, who I should have cried for. I knew something else, too: my uneasy misgivings among the

74

marble-white stones of Flanders were not illicit and unsayable. War wasn't dignified, clean and white; nor were the brutal deaths of these men. Of all of you. Now, of course, I recognise the impulse to grant you the dignity in remembrance that the last years or months of your lives never allowed you. But for me at fourteen, there was only room for one truth, one white-hot sense of pain and injustice. I'm sorry for that, too: for not realising that the memorialising efforts of your loved ones weren't a desire to falsify and airbrush, but to create for you the serenity and honour you were so cruelly denied.

Now every year, I wear two poppies: red for remembrance, white in the hope that one day no more of you will have to die. I try to look with generosity on everybody who remembers you, to recognise that really we're all just muddling through our attempts to make sense of the horror. On November 11th, I bow my head and feel everything I needed to feel in Belgium ten years ago. But I always make sure I have my poppies, and some time for silence, on November 4th: the day Wilfred Owen died in 1918. It's my way of remembering that the end of the war came too late for so many of you. For that, above all, I'm sorry.

Kirsty

Kirsty Rachael Heyam
24, York, Student

It's for everyone, but especially Wilfred Owen, for making me realise why.

Dear Great-Uncle Fred

Thank you very much for the postcards you sent back to Northampton. They're beautiful – little sheets of embroidered silk glued into cardboard frames – flags and flowers, a butterfly with the Union Jack on one wing and the Tricolore on the other, a crucifix, a cottage, the Badge of the Royal Sussex Regiment. On each one some uplifting phrase is stitched in capitals or cursive: *God Bless You … Happy New Year … Entente Cordiale … To My Dear Sister … Home Sweet Home …* I find it hard to believe such things came from a battlefield. I guess there must have been French and Belgian women working with needles and thimbles in clean, quiet rooms somewhere far from the mud and the guns.

You're fifteen. Or sixteen. We'll never know for sure. You lied about your age so you could join up early, and all the other records have been lost. You'll be dead within the year.

I wish you'd said more. 'From Fred to Nell, hoping you are in the best of health,' you've written on the back of one card. 'From Fred to Mother, 3/12/16,' you've written on another. Most of the cards are blank. Did you have nothing to say? Or too much? Were you under orders? Or did you not want to worry everyone back home?

Now ninety-eight years have passed and this is all we have left of you, fourteen cards mounted under glass in a dark wooden frame standing in the corner of my room in Oxford. And in the centre of the cards a sepia portrait of a teenager in uniform – bright buttons, big collar, black hair brilliantined and parted. At first glance you could be anyone's great-uncle, but if I look hard I can just about see something of myself in you, that double twist of blood and genes spooling back through time, getting finer and frailer every year.

Remembrance ... Honour to England ... Until the End.

Yours,
Mark

_____

Mark Haddon
London, Writer

Dear Unknown Soldier

Yes it's true. The young men and boys are always sent out to fight the other young men and boys … by the old men. The old farts are too lazy and mad to settle their differences around a table. That would require sustained effort, and dent the arms trade of course.

I've recognised your beautiful face, with its whiff of understanding humour on the station at Paddington as you read your letter. I was again shocked at your beauty. I'd like to have gently removed all that heavy gear you're wearing, and gently laid it aside, so that I could see and smell you, alive! And know you like before … as you take me in your arms and hold me to you, as we have done many times in the past. No, you're not unknown to me, nor to the many thousands like me, who are just left wondering for ever …

———————————

Bette Bourne
London, Actor

Friend

How did you feel leaving your loved ones knowing you might never return?
I cried for hours after leaving them at the airport, thinking I may never see them again and feeling very selfish for putting them in that position. It was my choice to join the Military and now it could change the future for my family. Was I selfish?
Did you have a list of things to do before you were drafted in case you didn't come back?
I chose fishing and bingo, I didn't really like either.
Did you have fab friends?
I did, without them, who knows!
Did your family understand that being there changed you?
Mine don't and how can I expect them to, I protected them from what was really happening over there. They don't want to know the scary stuff.
Did you cry when you were on your own?
I do, not just for those who have been killed, but for those who suffer every day because of the unseen effects of fighting.
Did you ever tell anyone how you felt?
I haven't until today.

Thanks for listening.
xxx

———————————

Anonymous
42, Gateshead, Veteran

I wish to dedicate my letter to the unseen injuries of war.

Dear Bwana Ottley

My grandfather told us about your scarf. Your mother knitted it, sent it from England when you set off for the mountains to fight. You came to grow coffee on our land, staked out a plot the size of a province but abandoned it to march off in the direction of a line. Your people called our land British East Africa, and where your brothers lived on the other side of the line, German East Africa. You even marched into Portuguese East Africa to catch that Bwana Hun.

My grandfather marched with you, carrying your guns, sackloads of food, and your uniforms. He carried more than the sixty-pound limit he was promised. The horses and mules all died along the way, thousands of them. You vomited together from the stench across the plains. My grandfather and his East African brothers became the hands and the feet of your army. They marched twenty miles a day, through short rains and long rains, without hats or shoes, unable to escape because they were so far from home.

He was a good soul, my grandfather. He had a farm with two rows of maize and bananas, one of sweet potatoes, enough to feed the family, no more. When your officers came one day to round up my grandfather, they said it was only for a month, until the next new moon, or the moon after. They walked him to a shed. An officer inked his thumb, took a print, and gave him a number.

That shed where your officers gathered so many grandfathers from our land became known as Carrier Corps. Some East African towns still bear that name. I live in an area called Kariakor.

My grandfather said you were better than some of the others. You once thanked him when he saved you two bananas. You liked our bananas. When your officers decided bananas required too much energy to carry because half the weight was wasted on the skins and stalks, and because they rotted in four days, unlike millet and maize meal, you almost cried. You learnt four words of Swahili, and you learnt my grandfather's name. When you wanted a cup of tea in the mornings you muddled his name with the word for teapot. You called him Birika instead of Bakari.

Sometimes my grandfather wondered what you were thinking as you lay down to sleep, hugging your scarf. You were a young man, like him. Once he thought he saw a tear. He had never seen a British tear.

Together, you marched half the length of our continent. You marched in long lines and required constant feeding. Our grandfathers were sick. They were as exhausted as our fields, empty as our villages.

Your officers never learnt or repented. By the time my father became a man, your sons were ready to call him up for your next fight.

Sometimes my grandfather became silent, he could talk no more.

Bakari ya Thatu
Nairobi

———————

Azmeena Ladha
Exeter, Writer

The First World War was not fought only in the trenches of the Western Front. It was global from its outset, and extended throughout Africa. The first shot of the War was fired on 12 August 1914 by Regimental Sergeant-Major Alhaji Grunshi, a British soldier from the West African Frontier Force in Togoland.

This letter is an attempt to draw attention to the part played – usually involuntarily – by the millions of African carriers and soldiers across the continent who were coerced into fighting for European empires.

You know, Mr Andrews, I have tried to write this letter so many times over these last few months. Every time, it doesn't come out the way I want it to. But the whistle will blow tomorrow – it will pierce the taut whiteness of a day that has not yet begun – and as you know, sir, there's nothing quite like a deadline to get me writing.

You are not ashamed of me – I know that. I did what my conscience told me to do. I signed up to fight. I did so knowing what would lie ahead of me. It has been worse, yes – far, far worse – than I could have ever imagined. But my conscience spoke louder than your lessons, and so here I am. I can only obey my conscience. I know you will respect that.

I am, though, Mr Andrews, terribly ashamed of myself. Terribly, terribly ashamed. I am shocked and horrified and disgusted with myself. I have killed other men. I have killed men from afar, their faces sooty smudges on the landscape. I have killed men who stand no further from me than our faces to this page: I have closed my ears to the snatching, desperate German that bubbled through their blood, and watched them die, euphoric in my power. I have been mentioned in dispatches for it, sir; they have given me medals and clapped my shoulder and shaken my hand. I have felt my heart swell for killing so well. You always told us that we were all talented; that there is something inside us all that is great and good and special. I never found mine at school: it was never in the classroom, or the cricket pitch, or in house. But now I seem to have found it, Mr Andrews, out here in the trenches and the wastelands of France. And in those quiet moments when the barrage stills, and time stops, and the world turns again on its axis, I find myself sickened by this talent, and so sickened by myself.

And so I cherish the fact that you are not ashamed of me, Mr Andrews. I need to believe that, at any rate: being out here has made me feel so desperately ashamed of myself, that I struggle, rather, to carry on. I know I will, of course – I must; I can't let on – but it is hard, and gets harder every day. I only hope that one day, sir, you will allow me to come back to school to see you. I would like to walk down that blasted slippery corridor by Centre Library with you and perhaps have a cup of tea. I would like to speak to you one more time, to talk through these last few years so that maybe I can try to understand it all. I need to understand what my conscience wanted me to do, and why. I'm not sure why I think you have all the answers! But it was you who made me aware of what my conscience was; it was you who made me aware of what I sounded like. I suppose I hope that it is also you who can help me decipher my own voice, and so help me explain why I have taken the decisions that I have, and perhaps lead me to a place where I might be able to forgive myself.

It's probably asking a bit much, sir. If I'm honest, a cup of tea and a sit down with you would be enough to do me the world of good. I always seemed to see better when you were around.

I remain, Mr Andrews,
Your most affectionate student and old scholar.

––––––––––––––

Alistair Boucher
32, Huddersfield, Teacher, Ackworth School

Dear Tommy

I planted poppies for my elderly father last month in a corner of the graveyard in the village where he lives. He wanted to show his respect for you and the soldiers who gave so much – to show that we have not forgotten your sacrifice. His own father worked down in the pits and was spared the horror and terror and, to some extent, the loss.

I cannot even begin to imagine what you went through, Tommy. I do not want to imagine.

I remember old men when I was a child in the 1960s. They were mostly silent, but dignified. There is not a one of them left, Tommy, and I am sad that I did not understand what it was that they had seen and done. I am sad that they were not honoured enough whilst they lived – those that were lucky enough to survive.

I remember my own grandfather, Joseph Todd, who served both in the navy and the infant Royal Air Force. He dropped bombs from a Handley Page over Germany and longed for the day when these great machines would carry honest commercial cargoes. He prayed before dispatching every bomb – for peace and for forgiveness.

Your burden, Tommy, was so great.

We do not remember the 'death-haunted days' which my Grandfather spoke of in sermons many years later, but I would like you to know what he said because I cannot say it better:

'We who remember the death-haunted days – we who have seen God's lovely sky ablaze – with fans of flame that raked our tranquil nights, searching the stars with monstrous rays. We have known that pain too deep for tears. We who have seen some dear loved name carved on a cenotaph and mocked with fame. What can we give for that vast sacrifice? Paid – in the good clean coinage of their youth.

'They went with songs to the battle; eyes steady and aglow. Have we dared to face that awful truth? We who remember – we can kneel and pray for the right to work in peace and live – fired with this Love we will hoist our banners – fighting the bloodless battles of the world.'

I hope nobody minds me quoting my wonderful Grandfather. He went on, like so many of them, to face the horrors of a second horrific war. How many of us can imagine that, Tommy?

I wish that our fights in this beautiful and wondrous world could be bloodless and fought with words. I think that you might agree, Tommy.

And do you miss the rain, gentle on your face, the scent of flowers in the hedgerows when you were a boy, and the smoke that came only from the stubble as it burned each year? Do you miss the sweet inhalation of fresh air in the early morning when the swallows fly low over the fields to catch insects and the only sounds are those of the birds, the wind in the silver birch and the river gently flowing?

Was it worth it, Tommy? It was for us, but it was a sacrifice too far, one that no one of my generation could imagine or contemplate.

Thank you, Tommy, for my tomorrows when you had none.

God bless you.

––––––––––––––

Elizabeth
55, Swindon, Housewife

My father wanted to mark the centenary of the outbreak of the Great War. It made me think about his father and my mother's father, both quiet men who served their country in different ways. I would dedicate this letter to Hugh Beldon Musgrove and Joseph Mordue Todd.

The poppies in the hedgerows this year are so beautiful and terrible a reminder of all the lives lost in order that we could live in a better world, which I believe we do. The only sadness is that the younger generations do not understand what was given and how rich they are as a result.

Boots on the Cenotaph

They weren't there when I went past before,
but here, now, on the steps of the cenotaph
were the boots of the unknown soldier.
They could have belonged to the *Big Issue* Seller
or a member of the Army of the Homeless but there was
    nobody else around.
So I could only surmise that these were the boots
worn by lions led by donkeys
at Mons, Ypres, Gallipoli and Passchendaele where 13,000
    men were lost in three hours.
Haig's comment was 'Mostly gamekeepers and servants.'
These were the boots taken off at Talbot House
and placed on the table to bring bad luck to all that wore
    them.
Each one of the Accrington Pals wore these boots.
These boots were worn whilst digging trenches, whilst
    kicking rats and knocking in fences.
These were the boots that scrambled over the top at the blast
    of the shrill whistle.
These were the boots that they were buried in but somehow
    they have found their way back across the Channel and
    worked their way through the concrete for us to realise
that they were real men
that wore them.

———————

Dafydd Williams
48, Cardiff, Red Button Theatre & Film Co-Operative,
Playwright

I dedicate this poem to my Great-Uncles Dafydd and Tommy who both fought on the beaches of Gallipoli, one for the British and the other for the Anzac Army. They were brothers and didn't know that they were both fighting on different beaches.

Alf

To say this week had been absolute torture would be an understatement. Of all the weeks that Dot could have decided to give up on her infantile ambition to run her own parlour, she chooses the one in which my hairdryer disappears. The oven has given up on me, so I have taken to living off boiled vegetables and Ruth's casseroles (whenever she can be bothered to get off of her rump and think about someone else for a change!). My own sister, too wrapped up in her own little world to even consider what someone else is going through. The house is a mess, and I can't sleep. I keep dreaming of you in the kitchen, drinking your coffee. I go to tell you to clean up after yourself, when the room fills with this thick green fog. It's choking you, you cry out and claw for me but I'm frozen. All I can do is watch as your lungs give up, and the green wall between us just grows and grows, eating up any sound, until all that is left is a deafening silence, burning me.

I wake eventually, usually in a pool of sweat. I think about you and our marriage, and how I never kissed you goodbye, or cried when you marched away with your battalion. We hadn't spoken properly for months, and I was always sour, sitting up at night, cursing you for choosing to be out with your friends instead of me – but I see now that they gave you the love I didn't. I see that our silences were shared.

But I won't take the full blame for this – no – because you hurt me too. I never felt appreciated, noticed, regarded. After a while I stopped trying.

This marriage had been beaten within an inch of its life; we forced ourselves to pretend that there was still warmth and love, when all I needed was separation. If only there wasn't such a slim chance that we'd ever be in each other's arms again; I'm so angry, Alf, that we wasted our days.

I see countless young men at the ward when I do my rounds; their hollow eyes, their broken spirits. They shudder and scream and lash out, trapped in sagging skin that shuts their agony inside, poisoning them until they are nothing but hair and teeth. If you're planning to come home, with empty bones and stale blood, alive but undone, your pledge of silence only broken when you howl at your fallen brothers, only to touch me when you resist my kisses and push me away, lost, my Alfred and his gentle ways cast to the wind, then don't come back at all.

I'm so tired of resisting the demise that will come without you. You must know my anguish at the realisation that I let you slip through my fingers. If anything, you must know.

Yours,
M.

Roseby Franklin
14, London

I have always been fascinated by the home during wartime; having the fear of loved ones dying every day is a true example of human perseverance and spirit.

Ferdinand. Archduke. Shot. So what? The lights went out in Europe. Our betters, our masters, their pride, their snaketurns. Our men, our women, our children ... our suffering.

I don't know your name Tommy. Neither do I know how or where or why you fell. Yet writing to you I am talking through the generations to a younger me. A snap of the fingers in earth time and there but for the grace of God go I. And guess what. I'm pissed off.

They play poker with our lives they do, all in on two pair. Preach to us it was all so, so inevitable. But ours is the glory they tell us, our sacrifice stamped onto medals. So how was your war Tommy? We all wonder whether we're up to the job. If visions of disfigurement, smashed limbs and death could be overcome or if paralysing fear would suffocate all reason, holding our hand towards the gates of madness. Was death a release from the bone-cold, weary wet misery or maybe you were hanging in there for the bairns? Run away. Run away. But they're clever bastards our masters. First they whip up a patriotic fever, over by Christmas, they say. Then they hook you with guilt and shame, your fellow countrymen are falling, you coward. And still there are some who don't heed the call. Call-up will mop them up.

So how was your war Tommy? Did they send you over the top? How many pistols were pointing at your back lest fear take its grip and eyes look back? Did they make sport of it and blow whistles should any Hun be sleeping on the job? I pray death came quickly to you, a bullet between the eyes, no lingering thoughts, no last cigarette, no calling out for mother, no pissing yourself. Einstein said the definition of stupidity is to repeat the same thing over and over and expect a different result. So over the top you went ... again.

Now you've fallen I suppose you'd like to know it was not all in vain. Well, the war to end all wars, ironically, gave birth to an even greater, more sickening slaughter. You were failed on the battlefield and the peace table too. There's no Empire now and still we fight around the globe and still we hear we're under threat. Nothing's changed there. And what of home? After a hundred years we have progressed, we are better off, our material lives have improved. However, our kin are still schooled to factory fodder level. Our role models make mediocrity an aspiration, our communities are fractured and our betters still come from the fields of Eton and still they want to spill our blood to undo the mistakes of the war you died for. They still can't leave us alone but I'm sure they'll tell you different.

So long Tommy, I'll see you in my mind travels again. Tonight, in my prison cell, I'll close my eyes and lower down your flag-draped coffin. I'll get the pipers to play their lament, the priest to remind us we are dust, the gunners to fire off their salute and shed tears as The Last Post haunts the air while I let go of a fistful of dirt. And I'll look down onto your tomb and beneath riddled soil etched into timber I'll see my name. Just another name. An inconsequential, expendable name. And I'll bow my head to remind me we are as humble as the dirt. As humble as the dirt my friend. And I'll kneel on one knee to remind me how death freed you from the lies …

The old Lie: Dulce et decorum est
Pro patria mori.

And I'll push my eyes skywards and ask myself if you're free. And tonight, in my prison cell, come and say hello and maybe you can tell me your name. My name is AXXXXXF.

Anonymous
Chelmsford, HMP Chelmsford

Dear John

A hundred years, or thereabouts, since puttee'd, smiling,
singing you swung around and off and left that half-harvest
beneath a blue late-summer sky, since radio crackle
godsavetheking and (probably) idyll gingham picnic on
now-motorwayed den, or hollow, or lea below the
crumbling stones of the forever farmhouse of a century's
dreaming, since deadeyed muzzleflash trenchvomit
duckandcover duckboard rainwater muddycaverned
heartcrush longwaytothecrashinggameshellshock horror of
life and death as a TommieFred, MickeyTimmy, lost in voice
and numbers.

It was your broad London Jack grin, a chin like a giant
knuckle, astride with the early spade in your hands, tanned
in singlet long before the poppies. Or it was your hound-
hunted expression, eyes mute buttons sewn on hessian face
captured lifting dead JimmyAlbert on stinking canvas
during the ringing stop of guns. Or your distant smear of
features, legs, fingers in midair backflip, hot death in a
history book above a caption made of statistics and overleaf
perhaps to the poster which put the mad, throbbing idea
into your head.

Now executive grey cars hiss along sodden redlight
greenlight streaked suburban kebab shop strips towards the
orange-lit leisure centres where rubber plants slowly die and
no one ever thinks of you. In a suitcase somewhere –
Stepney, Stockton, Stirling – a fuzzy shot passed one night
after the matinee to someone called a sweetheart for
safekeeping, a receptacle for whenallthisisover plans of
wedlock, house, a fair allotment.

Now you are the syllabus, the curriculum, amen, the
starting point for wishy-moral dilemma-ing. We shall
remember you once a year, or at least an idea of what you

should have been, brave sardonic cigarette-sharing hearty yeoman that you were or weren't but are, putting down covering fire, moving like a pincer to rescue raw recruit motherboy from ripping barbed wire death.

You're a statue now, I hope you're happy with bureaucratic pouring out of soterriblysad and telegram for mother and we shall never ever. You sank into the mud – so terribly sad – and others sank into leatherseat oakpanel political careers, into excellent whisky, into the arms of unjudging wives. Hooray for you, they didn't get a statue. If in some smothering dream I could believe a home-coming home-leave to careworn wife before bereaved and momentary, desperate release, relief, retreat some toddling version blinked back the tears near to the day two-years when told you'd never come back again then you know that he was due to follow you to the flashing fire, glittering guns, the game, the game.

Well John, I must be going – there are things to do and some things never change. There's a war in Syria and the other day I saw a man curled flying back, separated by miles and inches, suspended between the ground and sky, and I thought for a moment it was you.

Best,
Stuart Fink

Stuart Fink
32, Hornchurch, The Albany School, Teacher

A lot of our students are writing these letters and I thought I'd like to as well.

Do you love me?
If you are shy to say, just write, YES.
You might write NO, but if you do, please cross it out!
Like this,
~~No~~
And wait to see if you change your mind. Like this,
~~No~~ YES.
I couldn't bear it if you were to write,
~~YES YES YES~~
That's how I feel about war.
I want war to be written like this,
~~WAR~~

The children ask me if you sleep with a blanket.
I always say YES.
I tell them that you are warm and that you have jam on your
    toast every morning.
Do you think it is right to lie to our children about war?
We do not want to learn how to live without you.

Do I love you?
Yes.
Can you hear me? I'll say it again but louder,
YES!
I hope you can hear me wherever you are.

———————————

Deborah Levy
London, Writer

Dear Alfred

This is the grandson you've never met – Andrew. I am now 66 years old, and I too was a soldier, serving in some conflicts, but none as terrible as yours. You fell in 1915 in Gallipoli, with thousands of your friends and mates in the Regiment.

I would dearly love to have known you and chatted to you about your life. My dad was a soldier too serving in all the major battles of the war after your one including D-Day, Alamein and Dunkirk. You would have been proud of him, but he was only 4 when you died.

My son is a soldier now and has served in Iraq, and Afghanistan … I am so proud of him and all his soldiers in how they face the dangers of today.

Next year I am coming to visit you in Gallipoli at the Cape Helles memorial, so stay there! and wait for me and my group – there will be about 30 of us including some children and serving soldiers from the Regiment … we can't wait to tell you all about ourselves, and you will see how much we admire you, and what you did. I'm bringing a piper and bugler and you will love their playing.

With much love Grandad Alfred.

Yrs with huge admiration
Andrew

––––––––––––––

Anonymous
66, Kinross, Retired regular army, Soldier

Dedicated to all the Scottish soldiers who fell in the Great War.

London, July 1946

Well, old dear, I plucked up courage to go to London and see that statue you was on about that was put up in '22, and I must say, I was knocked for six. See, it could've been you, to the life it is, in 1917, wearing the scarf I sent you and reading the loving letter with it. Twenty-four, you would have been, and us only wed four years before when I was sweet sixteen.

You would of gone before but I cried and pleaded so much and to begin with it was only if you was under twenty-one. Then they started to make different rules when they saw how it was. So when the time came I waved you off on the troop carrier with a heavy heart, and I know you had one too, but we didn't show that to each other, did we, old dear? And God only knows what you went through, I don't, and even if you'd ever spoken about it, how could I understand? Of course it changed the lad I knew but you never gave one word of how it was, and you was gassed and shelled just like in the song you taught me,

'We may be gassed, we may be shelled
But we'll never forget the mademoiselle!'

How we used to laugh.
So when things started to brew up again none of us could believe it. We rallies our cheery British hearts though and starts all over again, we thought this one would be over quick. But it drags on, and poor old England got it this time. I saw you stamping off to work every day, angry as could be, what with Plymouth getting hit and our girls working on the land and our young lad at my sister's in the country. And you was off in two shakes in '42 when they stretched the limit again, you old soldier,

you was fifty but you still answered the call for King and Country.

And this time they did for you, didn't they? And you never came back to us. They gets a second chance and they done for you right and proper. But you wouldn't of minded, old dear, it's only me that minds, even though we beat them, because they couldn't even find you for me and now you're some corner of that foreign field as they say, which is why I came to Paddington to see this soldier, cos he could be you.

Anyways, I have to tell you, our Jimmy goes to sleep in his own little room again, just like Vera sang, though he's sixteen now and wouldn't like me getting sentimental. And even if the country goes to pot a bit perhaps we might have learned that war never solves anything.

They think I'm mad, standing here on the platform with you, singing Hinky Dinky Parlez-vous. But some of them understand, and smile.

———————

Jackie Snowman
70, Great Yarmouth, Hickling Writers, Empathiser

Dear Anthony

You will probably want to tear this letter up but I beg you to read it. If you do, whilst I cannot hope that you will fully understand why I refuse to participate in what I consider an insane war, and whilst I know I cannot compare my courage to yours in going back to the hell of the trenches, perhaps you may come to realise I am less of a coward than you think me. You are not alone in that belief. On my few ventures into the village I have collected enough white feathers to stuff an eiderdown. Poor mother has, on instructions from father, who will not speak to me himself, told me to leave the house. I somehow doubt if she will send me off, as she did you, with a beautifully knitted scarf.

When I worked with the Friends Ambulance Corps I lived in dread of coming across you amongst the shattered bodies writhing in the mud, or enmeshed screaming in the barbed wire. But it was not, as you believe, squeamishness that made me move from Non Combatant to being an Absolutist. The reason I changed was because I realised that by choosing to do a job that absolved me from any killing on the front line, I was depriving a conscripted soldier from that possibility.

You told me that many of your colleagues have avoided killing anyone. Even that on occasion, when your trenches were close to the enemy's, you made a pact to shoot above each other's heads. I fervently believe war, which people do not seek, will only be made impossible when men who so believe remain steadfast in their convictions. I want working men to unite en masse and refuse to obey orders to kill each other. And that has to start with myself.

I would not presume to compare my suffering with yours, dear brother, but it has not been negligible. When I refused to wear a uniform a charming NCO threw one at me and made me strip off to my singlet and underpants and take a bare tent to the top of the cliff and stay there, in the snow, until I agreed to put it on. I was there for four days and nights until a doctor ordered me into hospital. Then I was incarcerated in Wormwood Scrubs, where I was in solitary confinement for six months, on a diet of little more than bread and water, as this hostelry does not accommodate the needs of vegetarians. We Conchies were regarded by the guards and other prisoners at best as cranks but mostly, in the shouts that went on all night, as 'rotten shirkers' and worse. Now I am to be sent to a labour camp where my dainty hands, that look so like yours, which are more used to wielding a violin bow, will be engaged in hacking stones in a quarry.

We are told this is the War to end all Wars. You and I are trying to make this come true in different ways. Please God we survive to see the blessed peace for which we both are striving.

May the Lord bless and protect you, my beloved brother.

Hugh

—————————

Sheila Hancock
London, Actor

Tommy's Scarf

Her tapped-out knit-one-purl
was a private Morse code
as much lullaby as distress call
between Field Service Postcards
from France. Her autumn spent
picking up and slipping stitches
to shoulder you from afar.
Today it is a coil of python
a slithering bundle of welted yarn
wrapping your jugular: a ribbed
belt of bullets machine-gun issue
pulling your bowed head to assent.
Then it was a muffler, her umbilical
shawl of twice-ravelled wool
that clicked and twitched
over many a clock-ticked night
into a candlewick fabric, elastic
boy-looped, long as a man:
a fleece itching with unsaid words
still warm with smells of her.
Did she cosset you, Tommy?
Fuss and mither you? Dab
spittle to polish you, tidy a wisp
of hair under your trench cap
when you defied her at last
and donned Kitchener's Blue?
Before this tasselled winding-cloth
you lay cat's-cradled in a weft
of barbed-wire bindweed
that snagged on her name and stuck
for the two days it took to die.
A jagged casting-off attended by

No Man's rats and bluebottles.
Your fingers laced around her letter
in a certain light, are skeletal
but stubby nails, bent eyelashes
and boy-man jutting chin, are molten
unresolved, alive in metal.

––––––––––––––

Siobhan Logan
52, Leicester, Writing East Midlands, Writer

This letter came out of a week-long residency I ran for Writing East Midlands around Paddington's Unknown Soldier. We spent seven days studying this statue in its setting and exploring how his experiences would have been typical for young soldiers, drawn into the 'Pals' regiments'. We came to think of him as 'our friend Tommy'. The tenderness of Jagger's sculpture, captured up close in Dom Agius's beautiful photographs, is strikingly familiar and ordinary. He's a boy from our street. He's a railway worker. He wears his mother's too-big scarf and reads her letter over and over. Yet some of those black-and-white images of light on metal seemed to merge this human figure with the machine of war. Unspeakable things were done to this boy, more by his own side than the 'enemy'. In a symmetry of cruelty, at the other side of a field, German boys and men were trapped in the same state-organised slaughter. Crying for help, for mothers, in No Man's Land in many languages. We do not forget.

Hi Mate

I write this letter to briefly thank you for your service, your efforts and your sacrifice which you and your friends made 100 + years ago.

Having served in the British Army for twenty-two years myself, I can identify with some of the things you have experienced. The boredom, the routine, the camaraderie and laughter, and all the other things soldiers can and do share worldwide as they go about their duties.

I thank you personally for the things you experienced and went through so that my generation and others didn't have to experience them. The fear, the noise, the horrors that were yours during the intense fighting and shelling of the war you were sent to.

I thank you on behalf of all my generation for what you done for us.

All the best
Alex Sinclair

_____

Alex Sinclair
59, Hereford, Security Adviser, Veteran

I served twenty-two years in the British Army and can partly identify with the Unknown Soldier.

My brother.

How sorely we have tested and teased one another through our years. How unlistening in our squabbles.

And yet how alike. You are my brother and you helped me become who I am. Restless for rightness and impatient for change.

Let us agree to disagree, as all siblings must learn to do. I am convinced of my cause, and you of yours. Our fights are not so very dissimilar. We each yearn for change and lasting freedom, and fight for a cause bigger than ourselves, something to outlast us.

In the fight for the Vote, my weapons have been my words. At times, our bodies have been tools of resistance. But I cannot condone the violence I have seen, just as I cannot condone this war.

And yet it changes nothing. You are my brother. My comrade.

Your (wayward) sister,
Caroline

———————————

Caroline Lucas,
Brighton, MP, Green Party

Dear Soldier

Did you enjoy going to school?

In March 2003 I decided not to protest against the British invasion of Iraq. I was sixteen years old and was sure that my friends and classmates who left school early to march through the city centre were just pleased to have found another excuse to bunk off. I can vividly remember agreeing with a friend, as we revised the key dates of the Tudors and the Blitz, that our government would never go to war unless it was absolutely necessary. No doubt you thought exactly the same.

Last month I was at a county fair. While I was there I met two army recruiting officers on the look-out for active individuals 'in search of adventure'. Apparently they'd had quite a lot of interest from local school-leavers. Did you know that the UK is one of very few countries in the world where you can join the army at sixteen? On the same day I met a grandfather who told me that although he considered it unsavoury, his opinion was that war was a necessary way to keep global population growth under control. After some stunned silence on my part, all I could think about were those young recruits who probably sat in French or physics lessons with his grandchildren.

Recently I've been thinking a lot about children in school, learning about our collective past, about things like unknown soldiers and tyrannical dynasties. These young people are our collective future. Sat side by side – future politicians & protesters, future teachers & soldiers, future grandfathers & fatalities? How can we persuade them not to make the same mistakes? Is that something we're even trying to do, or might we end up with another classroom full of students like me with a head full of facts and timelines, but no understanding of how it works in practice?

I tenderly regret the action you wilfully and unwittingly signed up to take part in a hundred years ago. I have learnt my own lessons from the action I failed to take in 2003; and in some small way I have tried to contribute to interrogating and challenging the generation after me to think openly and critically about conflict. I am part of a bridge between your past and their future. And perhaps, someone in a hundred years' time will write us both a letter to tell us how everything's changed.

Yours hopefully,
Roxanne

_____

Roxanne Peak-Payne
27, Bristol

I was inspired to write by the potential we have to change the future.

My dearest son Alfred

I'm missing you so much, as is your Father; you are on our minds constantly.

Your little sisters ask about you all the time, they adore you! On sunny days I tell them you are sitting out on the lawn polishing your boots, on dismal days I tell them you are most likely sitting in a comfy chair reading your favourite book … they are too young to hear the truth about this war.

I received a letter from your brother this week; he is well and in good spirits. Both of my sons in France, I can barely breathe for worrying about you both, I'm living off of nervous energy, you are both just too far away from me.

Are you well Alfred? Are you eating properly? Are you warm? Dry? Please don't be cross with me for asking. My thoughts are in turmoil imagining all the things you are having to endure, all the things I see on the newsreels.

I can hear you saying 'MOTHER! I'm a big boy now, I can take care of myself, I also have my friends around me, we watch out for each other, I'm fine, really!'

The thing is you're my baby, you may be nineteen years old but you're my child and always will be and as your mother I will always worry, it's part of my job to do that, I am also incredibly proud of you and your brother, giving so much of yourselves so that we and others in the future can have free lives.

Each evening I kiss your cheek goodnight in the photograph upon the mantelpiece, do you feel it Alfred?

Come home safely to me my lovely son, come home with your brother so I will have all my children together again and we may be a family once more.

Loving you always
Mother

_____

Sandra Lyon
58, Leicester, Mother

*This letter is dedicated to my grandmother's brother Alfred,
who died in 1916 on the Somme aged nineteen years when she
was eleven. She named her first-born son (my father) after
him. Alfred was one of two brothers who fought in the Great
War. His brother Clarence returned home but suffered ill
health due to being gassed. I wrote this letter from the view of
their mother and the feelings she is likely to have felt having
both of her sons fighting in France.*

Whistles

Hello My Friend

You don't know me, yet you do, I am the man and woman you passed in the street, bumped into on the railway station, who looked over the railings on the ship to France. We exchanged a casual but knowing glance, there was no need for acknowledgement, we both knew it would be hell.

We met again in the trenches, waiting for that whistle; it's strange how whistles have become part of our life now, whistles of support when we marched through the streets so proud, whistles telling the train to leave, whistles telling us to disembark, now that final whistle whistle that sends us into hell.

Remember when we were growing up and went fishing? I can't ride a bike now because my legs are gone. Remember when we climbed the hill and could see for miles? I am now blind from the gas. Remember that whistle at the railway station? We were so excited. I only hear the whistle of the incoming shells now, the whistles terrify me.

Don't write back, my friend, because I am the ghost of the millions who have not survived. All I ask is that you read this letter, return home safely and make sure others do not forget. And when this horror is over and you feel the need to whistle, whistle a happy tune my friend.

—————————

Andrew Carter
63, Banbury, Carer

For my father, and the many like him who fought for our freedom.

Dear Sir,

'There is no one left here, only me
There is blood between my friends' lips
Boats are coming
The sea is calm
Again
But I feel like I've let you down, my friend
I saw your face, I saw your frown
The symbol of a million men
An honorary make pretend
And we've done it once again
My friend
We've done it once again
I don't know how.
I signed up, proud, like you
And now I'm sitting in the sands in the beach in World War 2
Wondering whether you
Ate the same food for weeks as well?
Did the taste make you retch as well?
Now there are only tins of cherries left for me
In sugared syrup, red and thick
Each spoon makes me retch a bit
I used to love my mother's pie.
But even if I make it back
Alive
I don't think I'll ever eat that
Again
There is blood between my friends' lips now
Red cherries stain their clothes
And it's only now I think I know
That look upon your face
Are you tasting the same taste you've had upon your lips for
    weeks?

My mouth reeks of cherries
They've never been less sweet.
I've been on the beach for three weeks now
Waiting for a boat
To come
I've written home, to my sister and my father and my mum
And you're the only one I've left to write
It's cold at nighttime
The sea is clear
A quick note I hope they'll find
If I die here
I just want to apologise that they did it all again
That there is blood between my friends' lips
That they didn't learn from you.
That death means so little to those who told us what to do
The ones that don't eat cherries here
The ones that point from rooms
And if I make it through
I'll tell everyone I know
That even sweetness chokes
When all you have to eat is this
And the syrup's thick with blood.
I'll tell everyone I love.
If I get picked up
And reach our land
The sea is calm today.
The cherry pips have sunk
Into the sand.'

Your friend,
David

Hollie McNish
Cambridge, Poet

*In memory of my papa, who ran to the bathroom to be sick
the day my mum made cherry pie for us.*

Dear George

We saw the memorial medal on the wall as we grew up:
'George Augustus Joyce – He died for freedom and honour'.
Gran would look at it and touch it with pride. She lost you,
her beloved brother, when she was a young girl, you were
twenty-five, and eighty years on, she still struggled with her
confused emotions because being proud of you would never
heal the deep sadness of losing you when you were so
young. Just as it was your duty to leave them, it was her duty
to accept your death without question.

When Grandad died and before she could give away the
little bit of insurance money that came to her, I asked Gran
if there was anything left in her life she wanted to do. 'I want
to see a mountain and I want to visit my Brother's grave'. So
we set off for that little field in France with the beautifully
kept headstones and simple words. She cried. On to
Thiepval and the sea of headstones for the missing of the
Somme. She looked up and said 'We never knew'. And I
cried. They had waved off their loved ones and had no idea
of the carnage and the waste of human lives. The sad thing
is George, we are still sending them off to die and the
families are still doing their duty by accepting the lie.

Now you have with you Lily Daisy, my Gran, and her
sister Eve, who named her first son after you. We never
knew you George but we thank you. Not for being a hero,
but for being a brother who was so very loved and that you
left that love with your sisters and for those who came after
you.

With all my love,
Denise

Denise Perrin
57, Frome

I was inspired by hearing about this project on Woman's Hour *and I remembered hearing about my Great-Uncle George, who was shot by a sniper on his first day back after being home on leave. I found a letter from his Commanding Officer in my Gran's treasured possessions.*

Dedicated to George, Lily and Eve Joyce.

Dear Edward

As your local Member of Parliament, I am more than delighted to respond to your concerns.

You tell me of the jubilation you and your brothers felt as you signed up to the Army together; your confession that you did so below the legal age (this will remain our little secret). Your mother sounds like a woman of truly loving devotion; I am sure she was weeping as much with pride as with sorrow when you parted.

I can understand why you feel so weary fighting at the Front for our King and our Country. The portrait you paint is so vivid that I can almost smell the stench of war: the mud, the dried sweat, the excrement, the tobacco, the quicklime. I sense that you still feel the loss of your brothers acutely. Their contributions will be remembered: that is my pledge.

Truly, I appreciate why, in the periods of nagging boredom you so eloquently describe, your mind has wandered to question why you are fighting. You fear that the sacrifice you have so bitterly experienced is for naught. I wish to assure you otherwise.

This war will ensure that Germany's sinister quest to dominate other lands and peoples will finally come to an end. It will safeguard the future of our great British Empire. It will be this war that secures a lasting and just peace. It will undoubtedly prove to be the last great conflict Man will fight, resolving for good the great underlying problems and traumas in Europe that have led us to this moment. When the guns fall silent, a new era of economic prosperity beckons.

So yes, I understand your fears and concerns, but please put them to one side. It may seem remote now in your world of machine guns and barbed wire and shells and poison gas, but the twentieth century will surely be known as the century of peace. If that fails to transpire – and it will not – then, and only then, would there be any cause to question the war, and the motives of those who sent so many men to muddy fields.

I believe strongly that the legacy of this war will be to demonstrate that trust in authority is justified, not misplaced, and that war really is the means to achieve peace.

Keep fighting, brave soldier, and all my thoughts for your mother; I hope they discover what ails her soon.

Sincerely yours,
Sir Henry

_____

Owen Jones
London, Writer

Dear William

I know I should have written you sooner. A lot sooner, in fact. I would say time got away from me, but we both know that not to be true now.

I'd like to think you understand, just as always, why I did what I did. You were the old sweater in my closet, the one that's soft and warm and just fits perfectly. I loved you. I love you now, still. And I feel that you must have loved me in your own sort of quiet way.

I know even now you'd roll your eyes at me for bringing it up. You'd slap my knee and tell me to, 'Zip it, Annie-pants!' and then you'd grin at me. That stretched, wide open, melon-wedge smile. But I have to bring her up. Naomi.

When I saw you two that night – on your birthday – I knew. I'd gone outside to find you with a slice of the cake your mother had baked. When I saw you, round the side of the house, I stopped. You'd wrapped an arm around her waist and Naomi laughed and pushed you away, but only gently. And then you both sat there, on the side steps, only just lit by the horrible glow from the windows above. And you had your first kiss with someone who wasn't me.

I know, Will. I never said anything until now, and you must be surprised. But then you are probably used to the surprise after I gave you that feather.

All those girls who had addressed you with one, and only mine could send you to war.

We hadn't spoken since that night – at the time, I just wanted you gone. I wanted to hurt you and Naomi and to make it all disappear. At least until Christmas. At least until then. That's when the war would be over, and by then you would have forgotten all about Naomi and it would be just you and me again. And I suppose it was.

Naomi cried that day you left. It's funny, I never really thought about what the white feathers meant until you were gone. They're a symbol of a poor fighter – a coward. But I think we both know that when I handed you one, I was really giving it to myself.

Your mother still invites me round for tea, every Tuesday since that afternoon you left. She's still a second mother to me – and mostly, we like to talk about you and what you could have been. She doesn't know about the feather, or any of it.

Like how the hole got in your lounge wall, or where we buried those awful shorts she tried to make you wear when you were eight – it's a secret that will just remain between the two of us, like always.

Always and always,
Your Annie

Chelsea Asher
22, Bath

Dear Unknown Soldier

You don't know me but I'm writing to you in the hope that you knew my great-uncle Claude Randall. If you did, you would certainly remember him. You worked for the railways but he couldn't have been more different. He was an equestrian, part of his father's circus act which performed all over Britain and Europe. The Randall Family entered the ring at a gallop, Claude's father astride two horses with his eldest son and daughter, Frederick and Lulu, on his shoulders, and Nell, another daughter, up above. But a few years before the War began, they had performed in front of Nicholas II, the last Czar of Russia, and shortly afterwards there was a bad accident. As Claude's father pulled hard on the reins to guide the horses to the circumference of the ring and stop them galloping across the middle, the reins snapped, and they all fell, but Nell, falling from the top, damaged her knee and was unable to perform in the ring again. Afterwards, the reins were found to have been partly cut through, possibly sabotage by someone jealous of their success. It was after this that Claude joined the act, and in order to replace Nell, he wore a blonde wig during the performance! Did he tell you how he would laugh as he sauntered out after the show, passing the young men waiting at the stage door for the beautiful Claudine?

So, this is why I'm writing to you. It's because I'm so angry with him. Perhaps I'm wrong to feel like this about someone who died in the First World War, but he didn't have to die. With his experience of horses, why didn't he join the Army Veterinary Corps? That's what his two younger brothers did, and they both survived the war, remaining relatively safe carrying supplies back and forth to the front line. Did he ever tell you why he joined the Royal Warwickshire Regiment as a private instead? Well, if he was

a friend of yours, you will know by now that he was killed
on 1 July 1916, the first day of the Battle of the Somme, age
twenty-six. I hope that his death was quick. But if you know
why he made such a bad decision, please write and let me
know so that I can stop feeling like this.

With all best wishes, and may you come home safely,
Yvonne (Claude's great-niece)

Anonymous
69, Brighton, Designer

*In the family history I am writing, Claude Randall's chapter is
so short, and I have no mementoes or photographs of him.
This is my only way to ensure he is not completely forgotten.*

Dear Unknown Soldier,

Even though people think your unknown, your not. You had a family, you had a name, you had friends.

All the people who think you were just a soldier from a town they are wrong, because some of them people who think that, they could be related to you.

You could be my great great great Uncle, You could be my mums great great Uncle you never know.

If you were alaive I would ask you,
Did you go to the war under age?
How many people wanted you to go in your family?

My mum said to me "we always tell children not to figh, but adults fight in wars"

So ever since I herd about you I wonder what you were called, what kind of family you had and what your friends were like.

I tchtnk war sholdin't be a real thing

From
Ellie   10 years old

Ellie
10, Egremont

14th Field Hospital
The Somme
France

Dear Benjamin,

There you sit, in the grotty ditch that we call a trench.
Reading this letter, for it be the last one I will ever send you.
You remember the day, the day we went over the top for the
first time. The Somme, oh the Somme. More blood was shed
on that day than when you cut your leg on that barbed wire
in basic training. Never thought I'd see it at war. The past six
months I have lain, longing to be back there by your side
counting the shells that fall on us. Things changed though, I
changed. The whistle blew, we ran, bang, I fell you ran. My
leg was hit pretty badly too. Six hours I lay in no man's land
collecting the dirt and disease into the open wound.
    Disease. It's the death of me.
    I've been told it's only a matter of time before I die, with
full military honours. But what honour? For King and
country that's what. Where was the King on the first day? In
a palace with no thought at all about honour. So here I tell
you, comrade, this is my last letter. I will die soon. There's
talk of another big offensive, so maybe I'll see you soon but
this time we will sit in a wooden chair, counting, not shells
but birds. One day comrade, one day my friend. Give the
lads my best and tell them to keep an eye on Sgt. Higson.
For I cannot do it anymore.

Matthew Burford
15, Wirral, 1123 Hooton Park Squadron Air Training Corps,
Sergeant

For The Royal Air Force.

Dear brother

They say there is a soldier who is unknown.
This cannot be you.
They say that he too was sent to kill or be killed,
For his rich King, and for his poor country.
But this cannot be you.
You live, you breathe,
And your eyes, the eyes of a survivor, are reading these
    words.
You are not unknown.

You are known by your mother who gave you life and suckle,
You are known by we who played games with you
On cobbled streets,
On broken carts,
On wasted land.
We were puckish children, in search of fun.
Naughty we were, naughty.

They say there is a soldier who is unknown,
Or known but to God,
But this cannot be you.

We love you brother.
You are known and loved in great measure,
And although you did not start this war,
And we who love you fail to understand this war,
(Damn this blood shedding),
We salute you.
You were called,
You were chosen.
You are in
The war to end war.

They say there is an Unknown Soldier from Ethiopia,
Will he bring an end to war?
There is an Unknown Soldier from Spain.
Will war cease with his demise?
Estonia has one of this kind,
And a Somalian cannot be accounted for,
But the soul and earthly ways of these unfound fighters
Are known by someone.

Many have fallen in foreign fields.
Their bones have been placed in tidy rows
Or left to sink in bog and trench.
They too fought in wars to end war,
But they are not you.

Brother, we wait for you here with those boiled sweets you
    like,
The girl next door still writes poems for you.
Your room is as clean as your dinner plate,
And your football team keeps losing.
Not much has changed.

If you see the Unknown Soldier show him love,
If you see the Unknown Soldier hold his hand,
Tell him that there must be someone somewhere who loves
    him,
Tell him no one is unknown,
Tell him that there must be someone somewhere who
    knows him,
As well as we know you.

Benjamin Zephaniah
Spalding, Poet

Dear soldier

Every morning, to this day, does your memory haunt a lover you had, as the war swept you away from them? Does a woman, does a man, hold your love in their dust-filled hands, or does your memory, your forgotten name, still stain the lips of their children? It's funny how war impacts the lives we lead. It's the facet of life that plagues the people, because we all want peace and love, but we are so strung up on being better and being powerful we lose our ideals in the heat of gaining more. In the heat of doing what's right, protecting the world from evil. I hope your memory never goes in vain. I hope the love you left behind, being whole and pure, was swept across everyone's skin you met, and to their descendants. I hope when the ash and when the smoke settled, that you were in a euphoria, that the love you had for everyone back home covered your skin, and you felt nothing but safety in your bones. Many years have passed, and your statue still stands reminding us of what war is, and what war takes away. Lovers, brothers, even sisters now, fathers, workers, shelters, people who cemented themselves into daily life and were then taken away. Time has collected the events of the past and has put them in books, in other letters, in telegraphs, in memories. These events will never go unnoticed, and the people who fought will never go unnoticed. You will never go unnoticed. No matter the time. We recollect the past from writing, because some of us were never there, and some of us will never know the true nature of a war. But you did. But your bones creaked in the night, your heart beat as the guns were fired, your ears heard the bombs, and the screams of others. And your statue still stands reminding us of what people have gone through, and what they will go through again, because the human way is one of power and demand. One of selfishness and gain. And

I hope your memory serves as a symbol for peace and love and a better future. I hope your presence shapes everyone into people of progress and not distress. You are loved, you were loved, and you will be loved as long as humans remain, as long as time remains, and as long as memory remains, your name will rest on someone's lips, you are not forgotten, you are remembered.

Love and Respect.
Mateo

Mateo Lara
20, California, California State University, Student

I think what inspired me to write this letter is that we forget that everyone who served in the past, and who serves now, was someone's everything. And they were taken away, and it's not to say they didn't want to go, but they were someone's husband, boyfriend, worker, friend, they were someone to someone else. I think the emotional aspect should never be lost. Yeah we have respect and admiration and pride, but we forget to acknowledge the love. I hope we never lose that. For people, the love and their sacrifice, like we dig deep and find our love for them. War is a tough thing, kind of an obvious point, and its aftermath is especially difficult and we need to be reminded, there is love remaining static even after all these difficult things. We still have love remaining for the people who were in the midst of a mess.

Dear John

I am enclosing a piece of twine. I cut it when I tied the tomato plants this afternoon. I used the knife you bought me. I really felt the weight of it. It's a thing of beauty.

Jack Barnes popped his head over the fence and gave me some canes, which was kind of him. There was really no need. I think he feels guilty. He shouldn't.

I wish I could send you the smell from pinching out the side shoots.

So, John, I'm sending you a piece of string. Please tie it to something to remind you of home. I don't know if you'll be allowed to put it on your uniform. I thought you might tie it to a button, something that you'd see and use every day. If that's not allowed, perhaps you could tie it to your bootlace. When you see it, it should remind you to come home before the toms ripen, John. Come home before the toms ripen and let's hope we have a bumper crop. We could eat them straight off the plant, and let the seeds burst all over our shirts and we could have a laugh and not give a damn. We wouldn't worry about it. Ma could come down the garden path to see what all the hoo-ha was and we could pick some more and laugh again. It would be good to hear Ma joining in with some laughter.

I keep hearing the brass band like they played when you went off, John. I keep hearing them, but they stopped playing months ago.

So here's a piece of string, John, and I'd like you to bring it home. I need you to bring it home. It's not a ribbon, John. It's not a ribbon with a medal on the end. I don't want to see one of them. I just want to see you.

It's just a piece of string, John.

Your loving brother,
Alf

———————————

Rob Walton
50, North Shields, Writer

Still reading that letter after all the years? You really must be the slowest reader in the world, buddy. Or is it written in code? Not really, though I suppose the bit where she says, 'I've fallen in love with Sam and we are going to be married' means, as Dirty Harry put it years later: *You're shit out of luck*.

Yes, it can take a while for the simplest bits of information to sink in. Only kidding. Obviously the letter in your hand is really an ongoing account of all the responses to seeing you in the long years since you took up residence here. Every time anyone looks at you they add another line. So in a sense you were the original interactive work of art.

Speaking personally, you were the second sculpture I became conscious of. The first was of Edward Wilson, on the Promenade in my hometown of Cheltenham. Wilson died with Scott in the Antarctic. And Charles Sargeant Jagger – who made you – also did the statue of Shackleton at the Royal Geographical Society, so in my mind you are sort of sandwiched between these heroic Polar figures. Obviously when I was a kid, on the rare occasions when I arrived at Paddington, I had no idea that you were made by Jagger but I knew about the war. When I used to go round to my friend Gary Hunt's house his grandad would drop his trousers and show us his shrapnel wounds from the First World War. Mine was the last generation that could make that kind of claim, who had that direct living connection to the war. The Somme wasn't just a historical event. It was something that had happened to people I knew.

At some point I started to think of what it would be like to *be* you, to be outside in a storm, wearing a soaking wet greatcoat. So it's good to know that you're sheltered here by platform 1. I'm struck as well by how few people pay you any mind. Maybe that's about to change because the war is coming into view again like a planet completing its hundred-year orbit round the sun. The present and the past – this bit of the past – are about to come into a four-year alignment. But the time when you and I were closest has passed. That was nearly twenty-four years ago. I was living in France, in Paris to be exact, waiting for news (of a book I'd published and another I'd finished, but trust me, that can be as agonising as waiting on news of the beloved). It was also, I realise now, the year of my most intense feelings about sculpture, specifically the statues in the Tuileries. But then, as a result of being in France, I ended up becoming very interested in the War and the way it was remembered and all the sculptures that were such an important part of that remembering. That's when I remembered that I'd known you for as long as I could remember.

You stand as a memorial to a mistake. So in a way what you're reading is more than a letter. You're reading the lessons of history. One of which is that, faced with the same situation, people would go for it all over again with exactly the same fervour. Because who could pass up the chance of making everything that had gone before seem like a prelude? A prelude to what? First exuberance and enthusiasm, then horror, then understanding. If the price was high that only emphasised the value of the lesson learned: that this was the war to end all wars. So that was great – for about two minutes. Then – oh shit, the war to end all wars turned into the peace to end all peace, and the end of one war actually contained the seeds of another even bigger one. So although we had learned the lesson there was another lesson to be learned which was that the lesson had not been properly learned – and history, if it teaches us anything, teaches that we will never stop learning. So *that's* why you're still here, still reading after all these years, still poring over that piece of carved paper.

Anyway, to revert to the personal (which, as you know only too well, is just the universal in a particular context), what I'm saying is what all letters say: keep safe, stay warm and please understand if you don't hear from me again.

_____

Geoff Dyer
London, Writer

Date Nov 1918

Dear Walter,
     Great news, war has ended.

Date May 1945

Dear Walter
     Great news, war has ended.

Date 2014

Dear Walter
     News not great, war never ends

Hey Walter
          Great news, you will never
          be forgotten,

Patricia Taylor
54, Colchester, Mother

Dear Ted

I hope this finds you well.

Your Ma has asked me to write this letter as she says her spelling isn't up to much. She's furious with you for lying about your age and joining up. She says for two pins she'd report you and get you sent home, only she's glad of the 6d a week you send her.

I turned fifteen last week, so I've ditched the butcher's delivery job and I'm starting at the munitions factory on Monday. It's long hours, but twice as much money, and lots of other girls to lark about with. They say your skin turns yellow but I don't care about that.

Garrett Lane is very quiet with you and the other lads gone – all the girls miss you, including me. Your Mum says that if you come back safe and sound you should settle down with a girl like me – what do you think of that?

I hope you are keeping well as we are here at home. Your Ma says she will send you a parcel for Christmas.

Yours truly
Olive

Diana Goldsworthy
68, London, Granddaughter

My maternal grandparents served through two world wars and inspired my lifelong interest in WWI. Ted and Olive grew up together in poverty in neighbouring south London streets, and left school at fourteen. Ted joined up under age 'for the money and out of bravado', while Olive worked in a munitions factory. They married in 1921. Ill-educated, they were employed in menial jobs all their lives, and died relatively early, after years of ill-health. But they were two of the best: honest, kind and proud; never asking, or receiving anything from anyone. And they were my beloved Granny and Grandad.

Dear soldier

You are most probably not alive now. You may have died at, or because of, the war. You have suffered, and you have sacrificed: your family, your health, your body, your emotions, and perhaps your life.

What you did not know, at least at the time, is that you have contributed to the most important change in the world. For centuries, sages, philosophers and religious leaders dreamt of an international assembly for arbitration and maintaining of peace between nations. The League of Nations was at last born. And yes, it may not have been effective, but it led to the formation of the United Nations and the Security Council after yet more of your colleagues suffered and sacrificed.

The world learns incrementally, and through the agonies of men and women like you, peace will inevitably be established, and future generations will remember you, and pray for your soul, and yes … will thank you.

Rest in Peace, my friend, my brother, and my fellow human.
Nabil M. Mustapha FRCS

Nabil M. Mustapha
83, Esher, Baha'i, Grandfather

I am a retired surgeon, born in Egypt, remember the air raids there during WWII, and treated so many war-related traumas in my days and in many parts of the world. I know how these traumatised people feel, just by being at a war and even if they are not injured.

Dear Unknown Soldier

The war you fought in, perhaps died in or were wounded in, was supposed to be the war to end all wars. Man, however, is a slow learner. Countless millions have, since the guns fell silent in November 1918, been sent to their deaths. Man's inhumanity to man knows no end. In this century and the last, it has been women and children, civilians as well as soldiers who have been the victims of wars, of genocide.

On this hundredth anniversary, let this be an end to it. It is right that we remember men and women like you, but I fear that the remembering is the easy part. It would be better to forget wars gone by and instead remember that the dead are the greatest advocates for peace. We do not honour you by these commemorations but rather shame you with our inability to live in peace with each other.

Yours in peace,
Gill

———————————

Gill Hawkes
37, Thetford, Mother

I grew up in the old Ypres Salient, my great-grandfather, grandfather and father tended the war graves of the first and second world war. These cemeteries are the greatest advocates for peace. My grandfather told me that war was the greatest folly and I dedicate this to his memory.

Dear Francis

Hold these words close to your heart. Let no one see but you. Daylight starts to peep at last so I can write. All night I've lain on the turf beside McCracken's Crag and beneath the endless stars. Remember this place? But of course you do. How wonderful it was! Remember how you whispered that the stars that blaze in the Northumbrian night are a billion miles away, that they existed a billion years ago? That we will go to them one day, that we will find folk like us out there. Like us? Imagine if they aren't like us – they have no wars, they are not cruel, they love the littlest life. And imagine if the other thing you said was true – the stars make music, they call out to us! I listened for that music all the night. There were the owls, the trickle of a stream, the squeaking of those starlings that crowd into the trees around McCracken's Farm. And yes, music – distant fiddles, faint lovely singing voices drifting from somewhere to the south … No sound of guns and war, of course. Except in the echoes of the long-ago bloody battles that once raged here, that have caused me nightmares since I was a little girl. And of those vicious mocking drunken voices that chased me from my home. Yes they did that, Francis, just yesterday as the day was fading. They found my secret. *What's that? What's in that bliddy belly, trollop?* Oh, but what a way to tell you, you, who should have been the first to know …

I will write it more calmly. We are to have a bairn, Francis. Does that make you glad? Oh, the baby seems to know I'm calling out to you. I feel it kick. I want you to spread your hand on me and feel that lovely little kicking life! Why so much hatred in the world, my love? Why war back then and war right now and war so deep in people's hearts? Why so much hatred of this little lovely life?

The sun rises above McCracken's Crag. I will wander southwards now. I will bear our bairn across the turf, the tussocks, the peat, the rocks. I will head towards the fiddles and the songs. Surely folk who make such music must be kind. Oh, if you could wander too, away from the bullets and bombs and not stop walking till you find us! Our baby sings inside me now. Daddy, come home, it sings. Daddy, don't die! Daddy, I need you! Come home, Francis. Turn your ears from the noise of war and listen out for us. We'll be where the music is. Soon I'll dance our baby on my knee and together like the stars we'll sing you home.

With all our love,
Elaine, our bairn

David Almond
Hexham, Writer

A Letter To An Unknown Soldier

Dear Unknown Soldier

No, not unknown as you were my adored Grandpa who gave me so much. You played with me, taught me to read before I went to school, showed me how to look for and appreciate the little things – the beauty of a tiny flower, the sheen of a bird's feather, raindrops that turned into rainbows with the sun, and also taught me how to make the best raspberry jam ever – on a open coal fire. Can still remember the thrill of getting the big jam pan from its hook in the garage, the outside blackened with use, picking raspberries under your careful supervision and knowing that the jam, made to your special recipe would be perfect.

Yet..... there was a part of you that was unknown – your days as a soldier in WWI. You never talked about those days and I never knew you were a soldier until well into my teens. From various snippets of conversation from other family members and a few things Grandma said, managed to put a part of your 'unknown' story together.

As a married man with a very young baby – Clive – who became my father, you went to serve your country in the war. You were at the Battle of the Somme, Passchendaele and

in the Middle East. (Still use the trinket
boxes you brought back from Jerusalem). There
were some very dark periods but gradually
with help from Grandma and people in your church
you became once again the loving man Grandma
had married. You were always in work until
your retirement.

You locked all the memories away and
never mentioned them, but perhaps some scars
still remained. You never liked people coming
up behind you or sudden loud noises. Balloons
popping were a pet hate - possibly it reminded
you of gunshot. You became a pacifist and
must have been so proud when Clive became
a conscientious objector in WW2 and went
with his wife to work on a farm.

Your pacifist influence was very great. Growing
up in such a home it was quite normal for
the T.V./radio to suddenly be switched off if
war or fighting was mentioned and as a child
it always puzzled me why we could watch
certain parts of programmes but not others.
(We watched the service from the Cenotaph
but not the march past). In some ways the
restrictions were a disadvantage as I knew
nothing about the wars. Wasn't allowed to
take History at 'O' level in case we had to
study a war. All I knew about the two

wars was that one was due to an assassination and the other started by Hitler. Never saw a picture of Hitler until I was twenty-one. Saw a clip of him whilst at college and asked my friend "Who was that man with the moustache?" She nearly fell off her chair in amazement! Needless to say, was duly informed afterwards. I never dared tell you or my father I had seen the clip!

Your death in the seventies left a great hole in our lives. You had seen many changes in your lifetime but you weren't really one for change or "new-fangled things". Can remember the struggle we had to get you to have a television. We won that one, but lost the battle of the telephone! You preferred writing letters in your beautiful copperplate handwriting and it was always such a treat to receive a letter from you. Don't know what you would have made of the seismic changes in society since your death but don't think you would have approved of such a liberal society and would have been very upset at all the conflicts still happening in the world. Technology would have passed you by - definitely no Silver Surfing for you!

I wish that you could have talked about your experiences on the front but know it would have been too painful. You just got on with life and left me with some very wonderful and precious memories of the time we spent together.

Thank you for serving your country so well so future generations could be free. You were never called on to give the greatest sacrifice for your country (thankfully for us), but many of your comrades were and they will never be forgotten.

Rest in peace my wonderful Unknown Soldier – my beloved Grandpa.

Your loving and ever grateful grand-daughter

Gwynyth

Gwynyth Joy Revitt
67, Doncaster, Retired

This letter is dedicated to my grandfather.

My dear unknown soldier

I see you when I come to work, when I go home to my family, when I am busy, when I am sad, when I am cross – but most of all when I think about my family. I have a family because of you and the many like you. People who went to fight, who left families and homes, and I wish I could say to each and every one of you thank you.

Thank you for facing things I could not, doing things I cannot even imagine. Thank you for you being you, and I hope that you could go home to family and that you and some of your friends lived to have a life. Yes, I know it was a life altered by the tragedy, futility and stupidity of war, but I hope you found your own peace.

But can you tell me one thing, please: did you ever ask why?

_____

Jacqueline Westrop
57, Downham Market, self-employed, Granddaughter

I would like to dedicate this letter to my grandfather, who returned from the war with gassed lungs and suffered his whole life, my grandfather who had a leg shattered by gun carriages and was expected to keep fighting, to my father who was separated for seven years fighting around the world, and my brother who has seen horrors that he will not talk about, and the women who supported, cared and worried about them and made lives for themselves and taught the children what it meant to be a soldier.

Darling Marilyn

So this is it. We're finally at the stage where just this paper brings us together. I know we've built up to this for weeks, but I never expected to miss your skin. That cluster of freckles behind your ear, the way your eyelashes form fanned shadows on your cheeks.

It's the little things that make me hurt. And it's the unknown, the silence of wondering how you're coping, the silence of praying for all of those poor, poor men. I try to tell myself that they're all going to be coming home to their loved ones, but I know, you know and they know. We all know the truth.

The thought of you facing their trauma first-hand is just too much to comprehend. Have you saved lives? Or is it always that little bit too late? Does the smell of blood ever stop making your stomach turn? It must all still chill you to the bone. I hope you can still feel something when you come home to me.

But, my love, if you don't – I want you not to worry. I will warm you up again. I will hold you for as long as you need, and I will remind you that despite everything that's happened, we live in a beautiful place and it is going to be OK.

Think of that. Think of us. Think of all that you are, that we are and will be. I will get you through this.

I am forever proud of you and forever yours.

Jenny

_____

Emily Duke
Brighton, University of Brighton

I call you dear, because you were dear. How could you not be ? All the life in you, all the words and thoughts and touches – how could they not have been dear? From someone, somewhere, there was a smile solely for you and then, one day, one moment, an end to every joy in that.

And, my dear, I am sorry, although my sorrow will not help you and alters nobody but me. I am sorry we paraded on without you and made a bad peace. I am sorry we condemned ourselves to do it all again – the men and women falling, dear lips, dear hands, dear faces ruined again and fire again and metal again and gas again and waiting and waste and hate and grief again. I am sorry we have repeated ourselves so often since you left us, varying our precise methods of execution, but always intent on executing, half-hearted when we try to build, to save, to love. I am sorry we continue to find each other expendable and that names are lost and significance falters. I am sorry we found it so easy to record how much your boots cost, or your rations, your buttons, your bullets, and found it so necessary to forget what was priceless about you, irreplaceable. I am sorry we ever learned the trick of thinking which can render a human being into numbers of various shades. Numbers do not bleed, or fear, or laugh, or kiss. They are not missed. I am sorry we embraced attrition and have never let it go. We simply hope that it won't take us, not this time, and will spare those we need, remove strangers. We run along the ghosts of duckboards and don't keep our heads down and we don't know when the dark will come. I am sorry that we couldn't learn from you.

I don't thank you for your sacrifice, because you didn't want to be meat on an altar, you were better than that. You were a man, which is a beauty, can be a beauty, should be a beauty, should be kept from pain and shame, from shocks beyond bearing and from being alone. I won't call you a hero, the meaning of that is worn away – it's a term that hopes to apologise for strategic and moral mistakes, a little gift to those who suffer. I am not grateful that you stopped being part of my world, that I never had the benefit of your life in peacetime: your legacy, your experience, your ideas, of the way you were a friend, or a father, a worker, a joker, a lover, yourself. I live in a hollower, colder nation for the lack of you.

I pray you are at rest and require no prayers. I pray you should not be troubled to forgive us. I pray all the good stolen from you can still flower, can still rise and be recognised and speak.

———————

A. L. Kennedy
London, Writer

Dear Great-Uncle Donald

It has taken me a long time to write this letter. When I started you were just one of fourteen names on the Island of Jura War Memorial.

You were hard to find at first, but when I discovered the 9th Royal Scots had called you up I traced you to Greenock, where your name is also on the war memorial there. The date of your death, 9th April 1917, led me to the First Battle of Scarpe and the dreadful fact that you were killed the day the battle started.

It did not take long to discover that you are buried in Roclincourt Valley Cemetery in the Pas de Calais. When I saw a photograph of your gravestone I felt my first sense of connection with you. You were no longer a long-dead relative about whom I knew nothing.

The news of your death must have been an awful shock for your wife, Janet, and your children. Did Janet receive your medals, the Victory Medal and the British War Medal; and later the Copper Penny given to every family who had lost someone?

When I started to trace more details of your life I was surprised to note that you were thirty-nine years of age when you died. You must have been shocked to be called up when you were approaching the age of forty.

As I continue my research I find that you left a widow and ten children. One hundred years later it is reasonable to suppose that all your children have passed on, but there must be some grandchildren still alive, and even great-grandchildren.

When I started writing this letter you were an unknown soldier killed in action a long time ago. But slowly I have built a mental picture of you and I'd like to think that through this letter, perhaps, I might be able to meet some of my cousins.

Best of all would be to see a photograph of you. Even a faded sepia print would be enough to bring you to life.

Today, as I finish this letter the only way I can honour your courage and sacrifice all these years ago is by doing my best to ensure that your memory will live on.

So long as that happens you will never be an Unknown Soldier.

Your Great-Nephew,
Archie Darroch

Archie Darroch
75, Dundee, Great-Nephew

I was researching my family history and discovered my grandfather had a brother about whom little was known. My research has uncovered a lot of interesting details; then I saw the Letter To An Unknown Soldier and decided to write my letter to my 'unknown' Great-Uncle Donald Darroch. It would be unfair to dedicate my letter to one particular family member.

Dear Soldier

I was born in 1931 thirteen years after your war to end all wars ended.

I remember vividly seeing survivors of your war begging in the street, mentally and physically injured selling matches. This picture has remained with me – always hoping this would never happen again.

Our soldiers are coming back from Afghanistan in 2014 in the same condition – when will man realise war doesn't solve anything.

Soldier you would have been so disappointed.

Rest in peace my hero.

Doreen McSherry
82, Hull, University of the Third Age, Great-grandmother

To all those who gave their lives in the First World War.

Son

Do not remember me too well or your mother's tender smile. Do not imagine our sunlit kitchen as you pile into the mess tent, or the lounge with its armchairs that embrace you and don't let go, as you shiver in the trenches. We'll keep a seat warm for you and your bed made. We will walk Toby every day. Do not let the memory of his pouting face and loyal affection distract you in your duty.

You are a soldier now. It seems so recently you were playing in the yard, throwing balls and rolling hoops down the street. Try not to miss the Sunday afternoons of football in the park but keep that energy, alertness and lust for victory.

Do not let these memories burden you but do not forget a single one. Keep them close to your heart beneath the scarf your mother knitted. Let them reclothe you when your muddy uniform has been hung up after a job well done. You are a soldier now but you'll always be our son.

Patrick Widdess
Cambridge

Dearest Brother

I am glad you like the scarf and that it is keeping you warm.

It is my first completed knitting endeavour so I am thrilled you like it so.

Today, I am wearing, as always, the lovely brooch *you* gave *me* at our parting.

I hope this letter reaches you very soon because my heart is aching sorely over our silly last argument.

I am so mortified that I made such a spectacle of myself on our own village station platform.

I am sorry we parted still not in accord.

My kiss was cold, my embrace was cold, my goodbye wave miserably half-hearted.

I am so sorry that I opined, in our last few moments together, that I believed war to be such a silly, wasteful, headstrong, dangerous, *boyish* solution to anything.

Such an impossibly *final* strategy for change.

You are committed to this war so it was very wrong of me to part not supporting you.

I am so unhappy in my unkind treatment of you.

I am such a very bad sister.

Since you left, I have, every day, tried and tried and tried in my truest heart to think the best of and truly support my favourite brother in his love of this war.

(You did indeed seem, on the platform, so like a lover off to meet his sweetheart!)

Since your departure, I have forced myself to imagine what good comes of it.

I have tried to see its best side, I have tried to change my stupid obdurate female mind.

I have searched the library for war's *meaning*.

Old High German *verran 'to confuse, perplex'* helps me not at all …

My Latin dictionary, which sees a link between *bellum – war* and *bello – beautiful*, encourages me to strive to discover its beauty …

The scholars I have consulted are divided …

Half of them see warfare as inescapable and integral to human nature …

Others argue it is only inevitable under certain circumstances.

Oh, why are we so apart in heart and body in *these* certain circumstances?

My dreams have been all of reckless governments, foolish generals, families torn asunder, horrible wounds, and, somehow, worst of all, boys deceived.

Understand, I commanded my heart.

And I have succeeded, in the smallest of ways I think …

I love you, therefore I must trust you.

It *must* be necessary for our future otherwise surely our wise guardians would have all done everything they possibly could to avoid it.

If *you* believe it is inescapable, then you must be right.

If *you* believe it integral to your nature, then it is.

If you trust that this war will make the world a better place, then so do I.

It will make things better.

It must extend our knowledge of life.

It must thrill and excite us.

This will, as you assured me on our village platform, be the war to end all wars.

Because you and all sensible men could only fight in it if it were so.

So, there you are. Victory!

The Day is yours!

You have stormed and destroyed the entrenchments of all my doubts and fears.

To battle, dearest brother!

You see how our disagreement ends in forgiveness and love.

And forget that foolish girl who told you, as you left, that she thought that to knit a warm scarf for someone you care for is a better endeavour than any war anywhere.

Your loving sister

_____

Bryony Lavery
Playwright

Thank you dear brother

For allowing me to live my life in peace, and safety. This memorial, in itself, is not enough to say thank you. But spending a few minutes here, and thinking of you, is a great way to say: Thank You. You died for this memorial to be built, so I could live to build it.

———————————

Dennis Gimes
67, London, Trustee, Soldiering On Through Life Trust, Veteran

As an ex-serviceman, I belong to the family of veterans. This letter is for all my Brothers and Sisters, of the Forces community.

My Great-Grandfather Henry

Hello. We've never met before but I've heard so much about you! Mum only has good things to say about her grandfather. You had a hard start in life. Sent away with your brother to a children's home by your own mother at only 8 years old is something I simply can't comprehend. And then to Canada at 12 – frozen to a horse and moved from place to place. I hope the families who took you in treated you well, but I know from the many letters you wrote your brothers and sisters that you tried to run away many times.

I know now your desperation to get home led you to enlist in the First World War. The Charity managed to tell your brother you made it to France in 1916 with the Princess Patricia Canadian Light Infantry or 'Pats'. It was a battalion for Brits – your first taste of home in many years. And so your journey began for real.

What a way to celebrate your 22nd birthday – The Somme 1st July 1916. I know my 22nd birthday next year will be very different. 60,000 casualties but you weren't one of them.

I know why you did it. I understand. You couldn't take it anymore. Who would? Too much bloodshed and too much terror. Too much grief and loss. I understand.

I understand you were scared.

I understand you did your duty for as long as you could bare to, fighting and surviving the slaughter.

And I understand you wanted to see your family again – if you could find them.

For you, a shot in the foot must have seemed a small price to pay to return to home, England, maybe a life at last. Even pulling a trigger for that takes courage.

I would love a day, a week, a moment to talk it through with you. I think we have a lot in common from what I've heard, namesake aside. I know you could take your drink! I know you never finished your education – but your son did that in spades and made you proud.

I know you were no coward, you were a fighter. Your efforts to survive are the reason I'm alive today. As me and my family charge forward into the future, I hope we will always look back to you our unknown soldier; Private Henry Benjamin Elliott. You faced total annihilation so that we can live in a stronger, new world looking for peace. This world is not perfect yet Great-Grandad, there are still many villains on the stage but also plenty of heroes as well willing to risk their lives for us – just as you did.

Those heroes have you to thank. Stay safe Great-Grandad we will think of you often.

All my Love,
Benjamin Elliott Barton

<hr>

Benjamin Elliott Barton
21, Warwick, Student

This letter is dedicated to my Great-Grandfather Henry, I didn't know his story until recently but I believe it should be heard at this important time.

Our Billy (or should it be Betty?)

Oh give over, what you need is a frock, some lippy and a bit
of powder to take off the shine. A nice handbag wouldn't go
amiss, neither. I went down to Paddington for the last time
yesterday and wanted to tell the gawpers come to pay
homage to you, *That's Our Billy and he were always trying on
Mother's best dresses when she were working late at
Gallsworthys and Father was passed out in the parlour after
hitting the gin.*

   You could get away with it when you were five but fifteen
year later, it'd become a bit of a problem, and not just
because you'd grown to twice the size of Mother. That's why
Our Napoleon were always trying to have his wicked way
with your legs. He couldn't tell the difference. Nor, I'm sorry
to say, could you.

   I know I was your younger sister but I felt so protective,
worrying about where it were all going to end, not thinking
you'd die fighting a pointless war that took an entire
generation of our men. I never married, Billy. Too many
women, not enough men, and I were never one of the
lookers. Closest I ever got to a man was you.

   Turns out you weren't alone in your *predilections*, neither.
These days some of them are quite brazen and they've got
this thing called, very rudely, the Sexual Revolution.
Women want equal rights to men but I thought, Our Billy
wanted the equal right to dress like a woman, which rather
defeats their argument. From what I can tell, it just means
women have the freedom to wear skirts that show off their
front and back bottoms. Disgusting. You wouldn't want to

walk upstairs on a bus behind one, Billy, or rather, *you* probably would – to get tips about ladies' underwear. Some of the lads even wear flowery trousers and blouses. You'd be in your element.

What I think is this, they can keep their equality when it comes to blowing each other's heads off. There was another big war after your one, Billy, which took all our lovely young boys again. They brought in these coloureds to replace them and started going on about 'race harmony', which at first I thought was about the fights that break out at the annual egg and spoon race at the village fair. I don't like them, the coloureds, and I never want to speak to one, neither.

Sometimes I pop into Middleton's Department Store, yes, still there on the high street, and peruse the dress racks, wondering what you'd like.

I've been given six months, Billy. It's those cigarettes Father gave us as nippers to keep our chests clear until we couldn't stop. It's going to be a terrible death, just like his. Like yours was, I suspect.

My last thoughts will be of you prancing around the house pretending to be the mistress of it.

I never laughed so much again in my life.

Yours, in this life and the next,
Ethel

―――――――――

Bernardine Evaristo
London, Writer

Our dearest Son

After a lifetime and a half of searching, we have at last found you. You are no longer an invisible face amongst the alphabetically dead, another body draped out to dry on the blood-stained barbed wire. Now at last we can honour the selfless courage of our beloved Sikh soldier.

We cannot begin to imagine how it must have felt to leave the plum and orange sunshine of the Punjab for the spectral black and white shadows of war. The cold trees that stood sentry over you as you lay waist-deep in mud and maggots, with only the death-tipped shooting stars for company as they spat holes in the velvet canvas of night. No helmet for you, honourable son, to protect you from the shells that whistled overhead. Instead you chose to fight and die with your turban, your faith intact amidst the shattered corpses.

We told you that the war in Europe would make a man of you, little realising that it would make you a hero. If you had known that you were to be baptised in warm blood and rain, would you have been so eager to serve the King?

We suffered drought and famine in India over those hard war years. Our crops died in the fields and so did our boys. We waited to hear from you; not wanting to believe that you were experiencing an even worse fate. Perhaps it is just as well that we didn't receive more than the occasional heavily censored letter from you. You wanted to tell us that your ears were deafened by the sounds of shells, your mouth silenced by the blood of battle, that young men of every colour and creed were being butchered like animals … If we had known all this, then we would have agreed that there was only one way back to the Punjab.

When we accompanied you to the recruiting centre we didn't know that you were heading for a land that we had never heard of, let alone that you would be fighting an enemy that did not even threaten our peace. You willingly fought for a power that occupied our own land. Yet that is the legacy of Empire – complete strangers are hurled into the cauldrons of war.

We will never forget you, our Khalsa lion, who roared into battle and surrendered his life at the click of God's fingers. We will not neglect your memory and allow your sacrifice to become meaningless. Your battle cry is the thunder that rumbles through time, your sword is the lightning that cuts to the quick. Your body may sleep, but never your memory.

'Waheguru ji Ka Khalsa, Waheguru ji Ki Fateh.'

Your loving Sikh family

———————————

1914 Sikhs
www.1914Sikhs.org

The role and contribution of Sikhs to the Great War has been sadly overlooked by society. This letter has been inspired by the pride and sadness of the modern-day Sikhs for their gallant forefathers. This letter is therefore dedicated to the unknown Sikh soldier, who embodied the noble saint–soldier tradition of our faith.

Dear Soldier

I am so sorry that, at the end of your life, you are 'unknown'.

How your family must have missed you! I can barely think of a more terrible fate than to disappear from the face of the earth with no one who knew and loved you able to visit your last resting place, and grieve your loss. I am sure that if you were my son I would spend the rest of my days in a torment, always wondering and wishing it were different.

I cannot know what you suffered, and I can only hope that you are now at peace.

The world is still in turmoil, people lose their lives every day in conflicts which seem impossible to solve. And so it goes on, loved ones lost in unimaginable ways.

And yet, to see you reading your letter, frozen in time, teaches me something. I will try to see the best in every day, to hold on to the moments of quiet happiness.

Thank you.

———————————

Sharon J
Stafford, Mother

For all unknown soldiers, and the people caught in conflict today.

Dear Frank

The May blossom's out here. Thought you'd like to know.

All my love.

Dear Frank

We thought about you today. I made apple pie and remembered it was your favourite. Funny how you forget little things like that for years and then suddenly it all comes back. Had to sit down and have a little cry, but don't worry. We're doing all right, your dad and me. Dad's started getting in the potatoes. His arthritis is bothering him a bit.

All my love.

Dear Frank

I know you'll be upset to hear this, but we put the farm up for sale today. We're not fretting, so don't you either. Your dad's too old, and so am I. And Susie's got her life in town, she doesn't want to inherit a farm. We're going to get ourselves a cottage in the village – got our eye on one already. Climbing roses over the door. You'd like it.

All my love.

Dear Frank

Susie came over today with little Jimmy. He's eleven now, skinny little thing, you wouldn't recognise that fat baby you held on your knee. He saw a photo of you and started asking questions about his Uncle Frank. I told him about that time you went headfirst in the river trying to land a big trout. He thought you sounded first rate. I don't think Bert takes him fishing, I suppose they can't, living in town. It wasn't so hard as I thought to talk about you.

All my love.

Dear Frank

Your dad's not doing so well this morning. Don't worry though. It's only the bad weather getting to him. He'll be right as rain once the sun comes out. Think he misses the farm more at this time of year, when he would have been harvesting, but he keeps busy in his vegetable patch out the back. I tell him he ought to be glad he's not trying to harvest in this wet.

All my love.

Dear Frank

Susie came by today, with young Jimmy. He's taller than me now. Bert's back in work, so they're doing better than they were. Jimmy'll be leaving school next year, he's talking about trying to get a place at the joiner's yard. He's good at carpentry, mended your dad's old chair a treat last year. Jobs are still tough, but we'll hope for the best.

All my love.

Dear Frank

They're talking about another war. I don't believe it'll come to that. Not after everything you gave, everything you fought for. The war to end all wars, that's what they said. There can't be another one. Mr Chamberlain'll sort things out.

All my love.

Dear Frank

Storm took the old oak tree down last night. You remember that tree? You used to climb it, you and Susie both. I can still see you sitting side by side on that big branch, your legs hanging down, and me terrified you were going to fall. Shook me up, seeing it lying on its side with its roots in the air and broken branches all around. Things keep changing, Frank.

All my love.

Dear Frank

Susie dropped in today. Cried at the kitchen table. I didn't know what to say. Felt like crying myself. I don't want to see her go through it, Frank. What I went through. Jimmy's off in the morning. Keep him safe if you've any influence, love. It can't happen again.

All my love,
Mum

———————————

Rebecca Harris
26, Corsham

Dear Darlin' Man,

– for that is what you are. A man. My man.

Presently you are needed to be a soldier my love, but soon, when it is over and you return to me, you will be needed to be a man.

To them, you are one of many. To me, you are only you, and there is not one other in all this world who can be the you, you are to me. Who else knows where you hate to be tickled? Or where you love to be kissed? Or how you want to be touched? No-one else. Just me.

Waiting here.

For you.

Only you.

None other.

Please carry me in your heart, and when it's so dark and difficult, remember the soft days and the sunshine to come. Remember that I shared myself with you. Remember it all, the moan, the sweat, the smell, the wet. Remember the tremble. And the yelp. Remember that we are alive together. The most alive.

Above all, amongst the black mess, remember the love. Let it fill you up. Let it be your energy and our engine. Let it bring you home. I am only some of me till you are here again. The rest of me is with you. Take a peek. You'll find me there.

Warm. Clean. Ready.
Only you.
Only you.
God Bless You.
Your Girl.
Forever. XX

———————

Dawn French
Cornwall, Comedian

Dear unknown soldier

You are going to die. It would be nice if your life was a good one. It would be nice if your death will be clean, painless, untraumatic, but you are in a war, so it probably won't be. You are very unlucky, caught in the cogs of a giant machine, and chances are, it will grind you into a broken pulp. You may have joined up voluntarily, seeking adventure and glory. You may have been conscribed against your will. But what you do now, what is done to you: none of it has glory, and if you survive your adventures, they will leave you a different, probably broken man. The worst thing is, it won't make a difference what happens to you. You're expendable, unknown, and soon forgotten. People will stand in solemn silence in honour of faceless shadows, mentally compiling shopping lists and twitching to check their smartphones. They will wear poppies and turn a golden-sheened mimicry of mourning into fashion. And they will forget any lessons your life, your suffering, your death, and your unknowability should have taught them: that war is not a noble adventure, rarely a way to 'defend' anything, and mostly, a shameful and horrifying waste, a culling of common people that enriches only the already rich and the soil. But you are unknown and forgotten: you cannot tell them what they should have learnt.

I hope that you have known peace before the war, and that you will know it again before you die.

_____

Anonymous
Cardiff

Dear Pte William J. MacKay of the Seaforth Highlanders,

Or William son of Catriona (Uilleam Catriona) as you were known in Adabrock, Ness,

We have never met and I've seen little of your possessions other than a photographic portrait – with you smartly turned out in the regimental dress uniform of the Seaforth Highlanders and the medal that was awarded posthumously for your bravery and loyalty. However, there's another connection that links us – I bear your name.

In my mind's eye, I have a clear view of the day you departed your home to face the bloody fields of France and the Somme. I see your mother, a young widow, standing on the barley field above your thatched house. She follows you with her eye and with the spirit of love as you move away through the heather and onwards to the village bounds, until you pass out of vision. Your younger brother is by your side, walking you part of the way.

In the neighbouring village of Lionel, you will meet with other sons of the parish to continue your journey to Stornoway, a sea crossing to Kyle of Lochalsh and onwards to Inverness and Fort George, England and France.

With a wipe of her sleeve, your mother dries her cheek and returns to put a peat on the fire – as her fingers trace the mark of your hand the tears return.

In the days that follow, sadness and longing weigh heavy on the hearts of your two brothers and only sister. Your bed needs not making, your bowl remains in the dresser without brose nor broth – your working coat hangs from the rafters and your tackety boots remain by the settle where you placed them, acting as sore reminders of a brother and son.

I should give you news of your family and how they fared. Your sister – my Grandmother – became a shopkeeper, brother Donald succumbed to Tuberculosis and brother Calum jumped ship in New Zealand. In a sense, your mother lost her three sons within the space of a few years. She was not forgotten. Brother Calum arranged for the building of a modern home to replace the original thatched house and your mother lived to a great age in the care of your sister Mary's only daughter, Christina.

Although a century has passed since the onset of the Great War, we have vivid accounts of the horrors and the havoc that you encountered – the turmoil of trenches, the screech and crash of artillery, smoke and wetness, mud and filth, lack of sleep and fatigue, disease and parasites – bloodshed, carnage and death.

I can barely comprehend how you kept your sanity within the perpetual hellishness of war, by day and by night.

I have a photo of the Beaumont Hamel mine that was blown at seven in the morning on the First of July – shortly before you advanced, with hundreds of others, to your deaths. I have another photograph of the Seaforth Highlanders' roll-call, later on the same day. What grieves me is that you are not amongst your comrades. Instead, dear hero, you lie lifeless and slain on the foreign soil of France.

Some five days thereafter, having said her morning prayers, your mother opened the door to a beautiful Summer's day in Adabrock. Streams of smoke rose lazily from neighbouring hearths and high in the sky the lark sang her morning song. Something caught your mother's eye. A dark-suited man was closing in – her chest tightened, her song darkened and the lark of her sky fell silent.

'As over it the wind doth pass' – and you away were gone.

Even in the depths of your Mother's sadness she did not complain – she faced her loss with fortitude and in silence like thousands of other mothers and fathers. Beloved sons and daughters, lost to a horrendously violent war in the name of peace and security for all.

If spared, I intend to visit France where you joined the fallen at nineteen years of age. On that day, I shall stand with pride and melancholy on the Redan Ridge where you were laid to rest.

To you, Private William MacKay, and to all the fallen soldiers, known and unknown, I extend my heartfelt admiration and respect.

I shall remember,
Donald William.

————————

Donald W. Morrison
Isle of Lewis

I haven't edited this. I didn't know where to begin so I just left it raw. After all, isn't war raw? It spells it if you flip it over.

'I just wanted all the wars to be over so that we could spend the money on starships and Mars colonies.'

Grant Morrison said that.

You don't know who he is, you don't know who I am and I don't know who you are. You could be anybody, English, French, American, Canadian or German, but I'm going to call you George. George Edwin Ellison was the last British soldier to die in the war. Cut down ninety minutes before the armistice, on a patrol in Mons, Belgium.

I'm writing to you from the future, from the year 2014, George – did you ever think about the future? – I wish I could tell you that it's true. That man stopped waging war and that your sacrifice made the world a better place. That it meant something. That it caused people to re-evaluate the world around them and how little we care for one another. I wish, George, that I could tell you that the Great War was the Last War and that we did spend all the money on starships and Mars colonies. That we as a species have spread out over the galaxy. That we now live on the moon and on the red planet and have mining operations on Titan. But I would be lying and I won't lie to you, George.

We spent some of the money on starships and we even visited the moon. People live in space for six months at a time on a satellite orbiting the planet two hundred and fifty miles above us. On a clear night you can even see the flashing lights of the space station and it is amazing. It's beautiful and amazing and a constant reminder of what we can accomplish. But still wars are waged and men and women go off to fight them and they die and then somebody else signs up and replaces them and then they too die.

I've never been to war, I've seen war on the TV, on the news and in movies, read books about it and even written about it, but I've never been to war. I have conflicting thoughts when it comes to war and fighting and killing for Queen and Country.

Sometimes I think that war is necessary, sometimes in order to settle something you need to show the other guy which of you wields the biggest stick. Other times, like with Iraq and Afghanistan, I don't believe waging war is the best way to go about it. War is a complicated mess of a thing, not that I have to tell you that.

You scrambled up out of the trench, slipping and sliding in the mud and mire, your palms landing in a congealing puddle of your buddy's blood, the cold creeping up through your bones, your fear a living, palpable thing in your chest, threatening to burst out and kill you just as easily as those bullets being fired at you will kill you, as the gas they attack with will kill you.

I cannot start to imagine how you must have felt, doing your duty for King and Country, for the free world. You must have been terrified but still you went. You had to though, right?

It was your patriotic duty. I'm sorry to say, George, but I'm not the patriotic type. If I am to fight and die for something it must be something I believe in, something I love. But for you and all the Boys who travelled to France, it was something you believed in. That's what it was like back in your day though, wasn't it? Patriotism and England Number One and honour and 'Damn the Krauts' and God and all that.

I think there will always be war, it's a part of our DNA, it's something we've been doing since day one and it's something that we will always do, George. We're good at it. No other species on earth kills each other like we do. The human race have made it into an art form. In your day there was gas and bombs and the dreaded machine gun. One hundred years later and we have unmanned airborne vehicles, drones, piloted from hundreds of miles away, and nuclear weapons that we can never use because if we did we would destroy the world. We'd finally accomplish what we've been trying to do all these years.

Killing every last person who doesn't agree with how we do things. We would also kill ourselves and our children, our families, friends and pets. Nuclear weapons will kill the wildlife and the grass and trees and the sky would turn black and blot out the sun and the world would die in freezing darkness.

We buried you when the war ended, George, in St Symphorien military cemetery, south-east of Mons. Your grave actually faces that of John Parr. He was the first British soldier to die in the war. You were forty years old and left a wife and a young son. I myself have a son, Thomas. He's almost two and again, I couldn't imagine leaving him to go and fight somebody else's fight. I'm just not built like that, I'll hold my hands up and admit. I want to die an old man in my bed, not screaming in agony in a filthy field with my guts slopping out, blood spurting all over the show, shitting myself.

I'm sorry, I know you're not George but it's difficult to write a letter to someone unknown. You might not even be English. You might be American or Canadian or French or even German.

If you are German, I don't hold it against you. Why would I? You were not my enemy, you were doing your duty just like George did his. You were just as scared and surrounded by death and insanity. You went off to war for your Kaiser and your Country.

Yours,
Neil Michael Burke, age 24 years and 346 days

––––––––––––

Neil Burke
24, Bury, Writer

I wrote this letter in the hope that my son never goes to war.

Dear Friend

In 1914 you, along with hundreds of thousands of others, volunteered to protect our freedom and – 100 years on – we still remember your bravery and your sacrifice. When you volunteered, you could not have known anything of the intensity of the combat and the miserable conditions that you would endure in the trenches; nobody did.

No doubt you served alongside other young men you had known since you were boys growing up together, but you fought valiantly with troops from across the UK and across the world – from the Indian sub-continent to Africa, from Australia to the Caribbean.

You will have witnessed immense bravery not just from men, but from women too. Thousands of women served on the Western Front – including the nurse Edith Cavell who sacrificed her life to save hundreds of soldiers.

You accepted all this as duty, you did your bit, and the whole country honours you. I hope that during your service there were moments of humour and camaraderie – perhaps you were one of those who played football in no-man's-land in the truce on Christmas Day – but I am sure there were long, horrible periods of fear, and pain at the loss of your friends.

The Great War will continue to serve as a reminder of the brutality of conflict for future generations to come – we remember you and the horrors that you experienced. It is also an enduring warning to those in power to avoid entering into war unless it is absolutely necessary.

Yours ever,
Ed Miliband
Rt Hon Ed Miliband MP

_____

Ed Miliband
London, MP, Leader of the Opposition

Dear Soldier

So many years between us. I don't know you, and you don't know me. But I would recognise your mother in an instant. Something in the face, a weariness of eyes, the downturn of her mouth. I have seen her in the supermarket queue, fumbling for change in her purse. I have seen her at bus stops, waiting for a train, walking down the street, her bags weighing her down like a terrible secret. I have seen her in the faces of colleagues, friends, of strangers.

They say no news is good news, don't they? But she and I know that isn't true. Whilst you were fighting for your country, she and I were waiting. Our hearts united by that tiny fossil of grief buried inside, a shell of amber held like a small shining rock. Our hands locked together, balled into a fist so strong that nothing can break the fingers apart.

And now the sun is coming up, and our shadows are tossed across the wall, and the family begin to stir. We will make breakfast, cut and butter bread, scrape the last precious jam from the jar, make a pot of strong tea.

And we will wait, she and I.

For the postman to come.

For the world to break apart.

_____

Kathy Miles
62, Aberaeron, Writer

I would like to dedicate my letter to my friend Glen, whose son has served in Iraq and Afghanistan, and to all the brave mothers who wait for news of their own 'unknown soldiers'.

Dear Brother,
Who were you when you left?
To fight, to kill, to murder,
In the burning fields of France.
A baker, a butcher, a postman,
Trapped within the barbed wire noose of war.
Killing and being killed,
For a lost cause known by none.

Dear Brother,
Who are you ~~now~~ now?

With hope,
Sam Greening.

Sam Greening
14, Hampshire, Bohunt School

Dear Soldier

It seems a very impersonal way to start a letter, as I write to you a hundred years after the start of the Great War. But I feel I must write, especially as I have just been talking to my aunt, Audrey Ridgway, who is ninety-one years old and the oldest person in our family. She would have liked to write herself, but finds the act of writing increasingly difficult and is not equipped with all the modern communications like the computer that I am now using myself.

In our family we still feel deeply touched by the war and the sacrifices that were made. By my side, I have the slightly battered writing case containing many of the letters written from France by the man, William McDonald Noble, who would have been my great-uncle. The letters were written to my grandmother, who lived to be 103. She had been especially close to William, her only brother, who died on December 31st 1916, and I remember her speaking of him fondly. She named her first son after him.

His letters make light of the hardships that he and others like him had to endure. But he also wrote of the things he could enjoy – and I am only too aware that as an officer he had an easier time than others. He writes of picking strawberries on the trenches, of the fun of having his horse with him and of the food and decorations they would be enjoying at Christmas.

Some of the letters make me cry. There is a little envelope with instructions for it only to be opened when the time came. It was not the possibility of his own death he was referring to, but that of his mother; he set off for France, knowing how gravely ill she was, while she was apparently unaware of it herself. He asked his father to give her the letter when she knew the end was near. In it he writes of his love for her and how he cannot imagine life without her. But he writes of his firm faith that the two of them will one day be reunited. He did not realise that this would be within a matter of weeks.

I am amazed by a letter written to my great-grandfather from Bessie Rankin, the nurse who sat with William on the last night he was alive. How did she have the time to write a two-sided letter? She was obviously deeply affected by his death and had believed that he would pull through. What a wonderful thing to have done, to write that letter. She told my great-grandfather not to feel he should reply, but he did, and she wrote back again saying that she could add no further details, but saying that they often went on a Sunday to visit the graves at Dernancourt.

Rather fittingly, a distant bell was tolling on the day when my husband and I arrived to see William's grave at Dernancourt. It was an almost cloudless summer day and the white headstones were gleaming in the sunlight. We were surprised to find four gardeners busy tending the ground. One of them was keen to break off what he was doing to help us find the grave. And as we got there, the bell stopped and the only sound we were aware of was that of skylarks singing. It was a beautiful and peaceful place, much smaller than many of the other cemeteries. I am glad my great-uncle lies there.

Finally, my aunt has a question. Are you the man who was indirectly responsible for William's death? If you are, we all hope that you survived and that you were able to return home and have a family of your own. We understand that William was on his way home on leave at the end of December. He was dining in the officers' mess with a group of men leaving and a group who were just arriving. The man next to him recognised a man sitting a distance away as someone he had been at school with. So William volunteered to swap places so that the two men could be together. As he did so, there was an explosion outside and William was wounded in his side by a piece of shrapnel. He died two days later.

I'm sure there are hundreds of families with letters and stories that have been handed down as ours have. But they still matter to us. You would find today's world unrecognisable in so many ways. Sadly, it was not the war to end all wars, but we still care about the same things.

Yours gratefully,
Deborah

_____

Deborah Jones
Ely

I was inspired by the letters written by the man who would have been my great-uncle to his sister, my grandmother. I would like to dedicate the letter to him, William McDonald Noble.

Tom, who sat across from me in Maths.
Jake, who built boats in the little harbour at Topsham.
Robert, who hid how bright he was.
Harry, who could be cruel.
James, who couldn't.
Oscar, who had the sharpest wit.
Andrew, who always looked out for Charlie.
Charlie, who became a father.

———————————

Anonymous
23, Lancaster, Sister

I thought about the boys I went to school with and the young men who fought in WW1.

They, the powerful, still insist it was *absolutely essential* to go into that war. The nation needed you to take up arms and get the Huns, for King and country.

You did as were told, went into battle, feet deep in fields of blood and mud, with comrades around you sobbing, begging for release. Or stiff and noiseless. Did any of them still believe the spin when reality hit them, cut through their bodies, pulped their parts and laid them low? I hope you cursed the top brass before you lost consciousness. But you were probably decent and a good Christian and very forgiving. Your last thoughts will have been of those you left behind.

My mother Jena, born in 1920, treasured a letter from an old relative, Abdul, who had gone from Karachi to fight with the allies. Dated 25th January, 1916, typed and translated, it was sent from France: 'Don't worry about my death. Only Allah decides that. And he is protecting me. Shells fall near me but can't touch me. This is a Great War I fight. For freedom.' India was under the Raj then, its people not free. And yet men like Abdul felt they had to support their oppressors and enlist. They, like you, were persuaded to do so by masterful manipulators. Abdul died of septicaemia in some makeshift hospital. And his mother died soon after, followed him to paradise.

When I look at your statue, I like to imagine your young sweetheart wrote you playful letters with rose petals in the folds. And that you blushed when your army buddies saw the red petals and laughed. (Young men do blush.) What I can't imagine is how she felt when she was informed – in that stiff, formal, military way – that you were 'lost in action'. In your neighbourhood you must have been hailed a local hero who died for a just cause. Such myths are necessary to keep populations on side.

Now, a hundred years on, politicians recycle the same old propaganda while jingoistic historian–warriors play war games on their pages. Worst of all are the authors and poets who romanticise WW1. One novelist told me he feels he's missed out on a rite of passage because he never had to go and fight, like a man should, as his forebears did.

If only you could come back and put them right, a ghost from wars past. At Versailles they left the Germans seething and totally humiliated. Nazism rose and had to be stopped. World War 2 was unavoidable. Some wars are unavoidable. But our nation seems addicted to military action. 2015 may be the first year since 1914, when British sailors, soldiers and airmen are not engaged in armed conflict. Ex-PM Tony Blair called out on St George's Day for a crusade against Islamicists, for him the biggest threat in the world today. Our people are weary of fighting but we may find ourselves taken into armed conflict, and an unbroken tradition will carry on. 'Never again' is the biggest lie.

Yasmin Alibhai-Brown
Journalist

For over ninety years now you have been 'on stag' at Paddington. You must have seen tens of thousands of servicemen and women during these years and I bet you have seen it all. Watching them rush off a train to greet a loved one, seeing them reluctantly walk off down a platform having left someone special behind. I have had to run past you many times with mates jumping on that last train back to camp. And you have seen the grim times too, uniforms lining up and waiting for their trains to take them to the conflicts that those men and women have faced since you first learnt how to put your puttees on. World War Two, Korea, South East Asia, Africa, Northern Ireland, the Falklands, Iraq and Afghanistan, the list is too long for this letter.

But being on stag for so long, you know all the places that so many people have forgotten. You have read 90 years of headlines on the front pages being clutched by the commuters as they hurry past you, hardly giving you a second look as they start the daily fight for a seat home. You know, more than anyone, just how much the British Army have given and have sacrificed over the decades because, mate, you are one of them.

That's why I wanted to write and let you know that just because the uniforms have changed, it doesn't mean anything else has. All the soldiers you've seen over the years have been just like you. They even use the same slang you did, 'Buckshee', 'dobi dust' and of course boring sentry duty, 'stagging on'. They also know what 'Dixie cleaning' means and that if they walk about looking busy with a 'chit' in their hand, everyone will think they are doing something important and leave them alone. I bet you had done that to get out of a duty or two! They also know the same commands to fight as you did. 'Stand To' and 'Fix Bayonets' still brings the same fear to soldiers as it did to you and your mates once.

They even talk about the same things as you did – home, family, what they are going to do with their saved-up pay. They most certainly moan just as much about everyone and everything because we all know it's the soldier's prerogative to have a good honk! They still carry pictures of their girlfriends in their wallets, and owe their mother a letter (or perhaps an email now). They still cry over mates killed and injured, and when they are together, where the real world can't hear them, they still ask what they are fighting for, but yet they get on with the job because, just like you did, they are fighting for each other.

Mate, after you finish this letter look up and find a soldier on the platform, recognise yourself in that man and feel very proud.

Stag On!

———————

Andy McNab
Writer

Dear Bill

I hope you won't mind that I have used a shortened version of your name. I've done this because I feel that I have known you for a long time. I'll explain if I might.

I'm now approaching sixty but as a primary school boy in Saxilby, Lincolnshire, I would stand in assembly with my fellow pupils every weekday morning. Directly before us on a large wall was mounted a grand oak wall plaque some six feet square, a memorial to those young men who had gone to war in 1914 and had not returned.

Distracted in school assemblies as youngsters are apt to be, I recall reading those names silently to myself. Your name, Winterbotham, was the last name listed. As a child your name made me snigger. ('It's got "bottom" in it!' I must have thought!)

Please forgive me for that minor indiscretion! For one reason or another, the memory of that plaque and your name in particular has stayed with me over the years. I have come to think of your name as representative of the many men who, like yourself, gave their lives for the benefit and freedom of those generations who followed.

I cannot ever know who exactly you were. I tend therefore to make a lot of guesses.

Perhaps you were an apprentice for a trades person in the village, or a labourer who worked on one of the many family farms in the area. One thing I am fairly confident of, though, is that you were a young man, just beginning to establish yourself as an adult. You will have had a loving family and perhaps a girlfriend back in the village who prayed for your safe return from the war. As a child you will have played in the village streets and lanes, attended services at St Botolph's church, fished with worms in the canal, and 'scrumped' in the village orchards, just as I did. These shared experiences somehow transform you into a real person who lived rather than merely a name on a war memorial.

I will end my letter of Remembrance here. In writing, I wanted to thank you and assure you that your sacrifice was not in vain.

The very last inscription on that wall plaque remains clear in my memory. It simply read, 'After many hardships, rest'.

People can but imagine what those particular hardships were for yourself. But now, Bill, may you Rest in Peace.

Sincerely
Colin Shields

Colin Shields
58, Sleaford, Nurse

The letter was inspired by the need I had to express my Remembrance to those who fought for our country and world peace in WW1. The Letter to an Unknown Soldier project was the ideal medium for me to do this. Thank you.

Dear Mortimer

I know I haven't written much, but it's not a bed of roses here either. We are finding life very difficult with you AND Bill being over there to say the least. You didn't have to go, neither of you. Now there's more havoc. You are going to have to be the one to decide how to handle this. Bill's Florrie, can you believe, has been having it off with that lantern-jawed old git from the greengrocers. He has to be sixty if he's a day.

The whole street is agog with it. You can imagine.

She's denied it all of course, but last Monday old Mrs. Clarke came upon the pair of them suddenly. I won't say more than that.

We can't send you anything at the moment, as we have eff all ourselves at present. Still, you might be home soon, please God, because I tell you son, I can't take much more of all this.

Mum x

—————————

Roberta Taylor
Author, London

Dear Unknown Soldier

One hundred years have passed since your war began. One hundred parades of the seasons. Spring, summer, autumn and winter, they roll on as they did when you were alive; sometimes kind, sometimes so bastard cruel they could knock the spine from you. There have been winters so hard we were pressed to put anyone beneath the ground, real jackhammer stuff. But I would not say that you were better off out of it. Not now, in the spring-turning-to-summer-time.

I am writing this letter on a train hurtling north. You would marvel at the speeds we go, over one hundred miles an hour and no one shitting themselves or shouting to get off. I am writing with my elbows tucked close to my sides because it is a bank holiday and the carriage is so crowded that there are people standing, squeezed together in the aisles. You should see the kit crammed into this compartment, so many bags and cases that the luggage racks cannot contain them. The guard is hiding somewhere, fearful of complaints, but no one seems to mind. Tomorrow is a free day and tonight the pubs will be full in Lancaster, Preston, Carlisle, Motherwell and Glasgow. In all the towns along the line and beyond men and women will raise a glass and wash the working week away and perhaps they will have one more than normal, one more than they should, because there is no early rise tomorrow. Even those without work may breathe a little freer, knowing they are not in breach of any obligation. But all that is yet to come. Right now we are crammed into this train, a bullet zooming towards its target. There is time to think and I am thinking about you.

Outside the blossom is on the trees, the lambs are in the fields, green grow the rashes oh and the sap is on the rise.

Things have changed since you scooped up your troubles in your old kitbag. There are no ploughboys steering horses slow and steady through the Ayrshire fields with a wake of birds pluming behind them. But the soil is still tilled, the crops still sown and harvested. You would know the smell of fresh earth (it filled your nostrils after all), recognise the calls of the rooks as they plunder worms from the soil. It must be hard to be dead in the springtime. At 5 am on a winter's morning we are almost all corpses, but sunshine raises the living.

Perhaps you never walked behind a plough. You may have been a city boy. Spring has touched there too. In Glasgow, pale as milk youths have taken off their tops and loll half naked on benches in George Square. Schoolboys are fly fishing in the Forth Clyde canal. They grill their catches on fires by the towpath, tip back forbidden cans of cider, sweet and tinny on the tongue, and boast about girls. Young men in offices feel the choke of their ties and will the minutes to go faster, faster.

There is so much you would recognise, but your jaw would hang open at the changes the last hundred years have brought. If you thought tanks and machine guns marvels, then you should see our weapons. We could blow this world apart easy as a child's breath scatters a dandelion clock.

I would not say that we have forgotten you. We stand in silence once a year (most of us), hold you and your comrades in our thoughts, lay wreaths of poppies at your grave. There are monuments to the fallen in every town and village. I have made a study of their designs; Celtic crosses, obelisks, carved arches, grim-faced soldiers and bare-breasted angels – your generation granted stonemasons a good living. Pages are turned each day in Books of Remembrance in every church and cathedral in Britain and beyond. Perhaps we would remember you more clearly if yours had been the war to end all wars but, for a man lying down in the dark, you throw a long shadow. Only the other day the radio announced five service personnel had died in the line of duty: *relatives have been informed but names have not yet been released.*

I have addressed this letter to you, the unknown but not forgotten soldier, even though I know you will not read it. The dead cannot read. The dead cannot do anything except moulder. You have a heavy responsibility, to represent all who fell in your war and wars since, because we cannot carry them all in our heads or in our hearts, there are too many to fathom.

It is spring and this train is not yet in the station. Journeys have their course and I will end mine soon. I shall think of you, as I trundle my case through the park, past the courting couples and the lads playing football on the grass, using the *No Ball Games* sign for a goalpost. You would smile to see them. This is not the world you left, but it has not changed so much.

Louise Welsh

———————————

Louise Welsh
Writer

Dear soldier

Please imagine:

A young man dancing in front of a military tank
A woman under the hooves of a royal horse
A million feet marching through the streets of the capital
A white poppy worn on a lapel
A balaclava-wearing punk in an orthodox church
A ship named *Rainbow Warrior*
A man threading carnations in the barrel of a rifle
A wall in Berlin smashed down block by block
A mass trespass on a Derbyshire peak
A man stoned and shunned
A song with mouth organ accompaniment
A mother shouting about the 'disappeared'
A girl arguing for her right to education in Pakistan
A family questioning the law of joint enterprise
A march of pride
An employee blowing the whistle
A cell on Robben Island
A dream
A bronze soldier on a plinth reading a letter that says NO

———————————

Angela McSherry
55, London, Arts Producer

My letter is dedicated to all of the brave people who find
different ways to fight the fights that need fighting.

Your Hands

Your hands never held mine;
they dug the vegetable patch,
skinned the rabbits,
they smeared my clean white apron,
finger-threaded your blond oily hair,
fastened your coarse brown uniform,
laced your tough leather boots,
waved as you patted the tail-chasing dog.
My hands held the heavy bundle
that told me you would never return.
Now show me your hands.

———————————

Bernadette Oldfield
49, Darlington, Writer

*It wrote itself. A poem for all women who have been left
behind – during any war.*

Why?

Why did you not say No? It's not a difficult word, Nein, Non; why did you all, French, Australians, Italian, Germans, not say NO!

I have never understood and never will, why did you all agree to join up, wear a uniform and fight, maim, KILL other men, your brothers and innocent women and children?

Because a Politician said to, because you wanted an adventure, to be a hero?

So what was it all for? Did the world change for the better? Were there even winners and losers? Or were we all losers?

Why could you not have stood together Black, White, every Nation linking arms and shouted NO! NO! WE WILL NOT FIGHT WE WILL NOT KILL! just because you Politicians, you so-called men of power, cannot get on.

Yes there are evil people and yes they do need stopping and maybe there is a God but surely he/she would not take sides, would not favour one Nation over another, would not condone taking lives in the name of Victory?

Both of my Grandfathers fought in the First World War: my Dad's Father had a mutilated ear from gas attacks and limited hearing and my Dad and his cousin who never returned fought in the Second World War. They did not speak about it, would not speak about it.

When I was a teenager my Father gave me a belt and a hat that belonged to my Grandad because I was interested in history but I could not keep it, it broke my heart to look at it, to smell it, to touch it. My lovely kind gentle Grandad, how could he have been a soldier, how could his son – my beautiful, smiley Dad – have killed a man just because he was a German and therefore 'the enemy'?

We teach our children to play nicely, not to fight but to share, this is OUR world, it belongs to us all, so WHY do we have to have wars?

Dear Unknown Soldier I respect and honour you and I cry whilst I write this but I shall never understand why you could not have said NO!

Tricia Lloyd Waller
61, Waltham Cross, Human-Being

To both my Grandads and my Dad.

Hello.

I must admit, I feel very distant to you. I suppose that's not
     surprising.
Time has separated us.
Your existence is like an echo in a cavernous hall down the
     road from my consciousness.
I know you were here once.

Every year, on the 25th of April, I've been trained to
     remember you.
As a little girl, I would wake up very early and go to the
     dawn service in ANZAC Park in Nelson, New Zealand.
There were the men in their uniforms, red poppies pinned
     to their chests, neat and tidy.
There were the plates of ANZAC biscuits, simple, dry and
     sweet (the perfect companion to a cup of hot chocolate).
At the end,
after 'the going down of the sun and in the morning',
after the last post, that sad solitary trumpet, craving jazz and
     joy,
after a moment of silence,
the gunshot.
It always gave me a fright, the gunshot salute.
I felt it echo through my buoyant, bouncing child's body.
It felt curiously cruel, ending the service the same way your
     life would have ended,
with that cold, sharp metal teardrop,
that bullet made of fear, used for fear,
piercing fear into you, fear into me,
fear into the world, fear into your family.
That bullet shot, that salute still echoes in me today.

I don't know what your eyes consumed unwillingly.
I don't know if you thought you made a difference.
I don't know whether you believed in God, in heaven or in
hell.
I don't know what you loved, or who, or where.
I don't know if you were Maori, or Fijian, or Pakeha, or
Scottish, or Irish or Australian.

Lest we forget, they say. And I do my best.
But I wish I knew more.
To me all you are is the echo of a gunshot.
You are defined by your unjust death.
I can only mourn the loss of possibility, and that feels so
dissatisfying.
How much you could have given the world!
How deeply ashamed I am to know that though your loss is
still mourned, there are so many innocent lives lost daily
on this earth in much the same way you went,
the same metal teardrop, the same frozen hatred that
pierced you,
it pierces people today, rips through their bodies, young and
old, male and female alike.
The technology might be different but the act is the same.
And once a year, I open myself up and feel that rip echo in
my body,
through every molecule, through every inch of me.
I want to numb myself to it, I want to forget it. It hurts,
remembering.
But you, them, they, her, him, you had no choice.
Yesterday, and today and no doubt tomorrow, we cannot
afford to forget.
We will, we must, with every fibre in our vulnerable, finite,
beauteous beings,
remember them.

In this flawed letter,
I have tried my best to remember you.
And I wish it were enough.

_____

Clare Marci Wilson
23, Glasgow, Royal Conservatoire of Scotland, Student

Dear Great-Uncle Stanley Clemerson

You were reported missing presumed dead after the Battle of Loos, a proud member of The Welsh Regiment. You signed on aged fifteen years in Cardiff, telling the recruiting sergeant you were much older. Your father was a hard man, he had already given you a new suit and a £5 note and told you to leave home and get a job when you left school at fourteen. You had gone to live with your newly married sister Amy Smith and when you told her you'd joined up she immediately went to the recruitment office to explain you were under age. The sergeant told her to come back with your father in the morning to sort things out. He refused to go, saying the army would make a man out of you. God help you, you were an enthusiastic child and you died in one of the dirtiest battles of the war. Your death created a family rift that was never mended. I see you as a frightened lad in a world of carnage hell, and look at my grandsons of your age and cannot imagine them in similar circumstances.

Rest in peace, dear Stan. God bless.

_____

Pam Clatworthy
80, Holmrook, Author

To my Aunt Sylvia, now deceased, who never forgot her young uncle and told me the story of Stan.

Dear Infantry man

When my father sits to talk of the Nigerian civil war, the
bravery that left him the year he suffered a stroke returns to fill
out his face. The first time he saw my mother he told her she
would be his wife and the same spark which she thought of as
arrogance, which she later came to love, returns to his eyes,
runs down his arms, inflates his chest as if his body chose to
forget it once broke down. The light flickering on his face is
from something called a laptop computer, which is like a
wireless with pictures – can you imagine that? It is connected
to the internet which is a vast library of everything we have
ever known. From the laptop, a man called John is singing.

When my father says a bullet interrupted his classes, he
means he was in secondary school when the conflict spread
across the midwest of Nigeria. The headmaster called an
assembly and explained though he championed their
education above everything else, death had come knocking
on their door in the shape of shells, artillery and gunfire and
he could no longer protect them. As if a nightmare had
risen from their history books, war erupted, unreal,
exciting, frightening, and my father mounted trucks
reserved for cattle to travel the rocky road home.

When my father says his street was shelled, he means the
whole town was levelled, he means houses exploded or were
burnt out, farms were turned to craters, the hills and highs
of childhood were made low and the crevices and hidden
places he'd known were reduced to dust. When he says the
town across the River Niger on the other side was where the
combatants were based, he means they had taken up arms
against his family and friends.

When my father says he used to row across that river to
play with those townsfolk, he means they were his
neighbours, which means they were his family, which means

the battle was brother against brother, which means the line drawn in the sand of the civil war was a river, which means the line was water, which means the line was blurred. When my father says 'It is the same old story', he means it happens in all wars.

The man called John is still singing from the laptop. His voice comes over my father's as he speaks of war. Years ago, when John heard the British Government armed the brothers fighting in that civil war, he sent his royal MBE medal back to the Queen of England. Though everyone talked about this, the palace said nothing, which is to say the throne shrugged, which is to say when families die in the blurred brotherly lines that is war, that is all wars, the generals and kings in corridors of power calculate, quantify and choose to risk the lives of infantry soldiers, which is to say you were an acceptable casualty of war, which is unacceptable.

When my father says his uncle fought on the other side, he means his family was in mutiny, which means his blood fought blood, which is what happens when you have a stroke, which was when the light dimmed in his eyes, which is happening now as his memories turn dark and John's beautiful song draws to a close. When father writes 'World War 1' into the laptop, we find out how many of your brothers died. We see how many wars are happening and the ones about to start. John's song is about peace and as it finishes, my father reads about past conflicts, about how we never learn from those mistakes even though we know how they happened. As he reads, John's song starts again singing over these accounts of violence, over brothers who have fought and died. My father lifts his voice to sing with John. Just Imagine.

Inua Ellams
London, Poet

Dear Tommy

You don't know me and I don't know you.

You, somebody's son, perhaps brother, husband and a father too. I imagine you marching off with your Pals to do your bit for King and Country, young, proud and full of life. I pray that you did not suffer and that the end came quickly.

Maybe you met my grandfather, Jack, he was one of the lucky ones. Wounded at the Battle of the Somme, invalided out, he was able to come home to his beloved wife, Lall, and pick up the pieces of his life.

In another war in 1939 Jack lost his life on the Mersey. I went to St Nicks in Liverpool to light a candle for him. Shine on Jack.

What is it all about? Power, greed, religion? Nothing changes throughout history. How pointless. All those people dead and still it goes on.

I know how your mum felt.

I know what it feels like to hold your son at birth.

I know how proud I felt at my son's Passing Out Parade.

I know how it felt when he was posted to Iraq and Afghanistan.

I know how it felt when he came home safe.

I know your mum, Tommy, and I know you.

We know, one hundred years on, that it needs to stop now.

You gave your life for our freedom, still the fighting goes on.

Shine on Tommy, I will never forget you.

With deepest respect
Shelagh

_____

Shelagh
64, Merseyside, Mother

I have the letters my grandfather wrote to my gran during WW1. I have a son in the forces who has a wife and daughter. Family mean everything. Respect for all servicemen who serve our country.

Weds 16 July 2014

Dear Unknown Soldier

Perhaps you knew my grandfather? I didn't.

Perhaps you were born in the same English country town as him when Victoria was Queen?

Perhaps you went to the same school as him?

Perhaps you joined up to fight together in 1914?

Perhaps you understood why you were sent to fight other young men like you?

Perhaps you were at the Somme together?

Perhaps you looked down on his life after you were killed?

Perhaps you saw the torment he suffered when he was sent back to the front?

Thomas Steven Burnham Lee
59, Crowborough

Perhaps you followed him from above when he struggled so hard after the Great War?

Perhaps you looked over him during his dark hours of depression when no one else could?

Perhaps you saw him take his own life on 25 July 1943 when the next World War was at it's darkest?

Perhaps you gave your life for the generations to come?

Perhaps I can thank you in this letter?

Perhaps you knew my grandfather? I didn't

Yours sincerely

Tom S. B. Lee

TOM. S. B. LEE
Grandson of Leopold Hubert (Bert) Lander
31 May 1886 — 25 July 1943

In memory of my mother's father following my mother's death in 2013 and reading her diaries afterwards.

To Unknown Soldier

Should I call you that? As such an important role to modern society shouldn't you have a name? I suppose if you don't it'll make it easier for people to grieve for you. I wonder who you really are; probably someone who got picked on for not going to war even though you didn't want to go solely for this one purpose of death. I guess we're all afraid of dying, even the ones who say they aren't.

But anyway, how are you? I guess there are a lot of people talking to you but has anyone asked how you, the Unknown Soldier, are? I think you should know that we won that war. The one you were fighting for; the first war to end all wars. Yeah if you saw us now you would probably be ashamed. I don't think I could stand this world being you, nothing is genuine enough, and nothing lasts. But there are some great things about this place. Phones and technology and even though the music has become worse and they don't really play that elevator music anymore, the place is still an amazing thing to look at.

I don't think you should feel bad for dying, you know if you're feeling things. Now you've not only become an important soldier but your significance has been placed into the hands of a very important pile of sculpted rock. Us humans; so sentimental. But as much as that is a fatal flaw it's also a key element of being human. And no one is calling you a murderer, or a gunman, an assassin or a killer. Even though if you were fighting for your own gain you would be put in every category, but war is suddenly the great excuse.

Did you know that being upset about the war has become mandatory? I read this other letter from an anonymous writer about how the two minutes' silence is something that people find a waste of their time. Kind of reminds me of advertisements when you're watching your favourite programme. You probably don't know about that sort of stuff either but I guess it like has to reload the weapon before you shoot, you don't want to waste that precious time.

Either way, you did one awesome job in that giant fight between more than two countries. Poppies have become the world war significance right now. Would you agree? To wear a flower that was designed and that you had to pay for just to support a cause that has already been gone?

Well I think the best part of this all is this; you my incredibly unknown friend have succeeded in life. You have made a preservation of yourself in where everyone can see you and everyone can talk to you. You are preserved in time and that is the greatest goal for us guys. People are crying over you man, they don't even know who you are, and that is pretty awesome. Do you think I should sign this letter off anonymously? That would make me unknown too and we could keep that tradition going strong. But the legacy is for you and you're doing a darn good job of it too.

So on and so forth, S. Khan

PS Would you write this stuff in Morse code? Would you just be like:

../ /. /./ /. /// ./ /. ... /// ./.. /.. .. . ./.

_____

S. Khan
14, Crawley, Hazelwick School

Daddy

I miss you so much. I wish I could click my fingers and have the war over with; and for all the brave soldiers to return home to their families and friends. I wish that everyone who had died in the war could be magically brought back to life – like Aunt Sally's husband down the road from us. I wish that you could be able to watch me in my school play or that you could stop Mummy crying.

I cry too, but I don't cry because I miss you like mummy does. I cried when I didn't get picked for the main role in our school play and I cried when Charlie pushed me over and I grazed my knee, however I don't cry because I miss you. I don't cry because I know in my heart that I will see you again; so why waste the tears when people like Aunt Sally need them more.

I want you back with me and Mummy but I know you have to do your job and I am so so so proud of you and when you can finally come home I'm going to give you the biggest hug ever! I remember when you told me that you were going to war, I was so shocked and sad. I remember you picking my head up and saying 'Always keep your head up no matter what baby' and gave me a kiss. In that moment you made me feel safer and happier; all of my anger turned to pride.

Thank you Daddy,
love Nathalie.
p.s. always keep your head up.

Nathalie Stocks
14, Bromley, Newstead Wood, Student

I would like to dedicate this to my dad who was stationed in Afghanistan. He died seven months ago and I miss him more and more every day.

Handsome, you've done your job.

The committee that commissioned you explained to the artist that a good war memorial should provoke the emotions of Pride, Sadness and Fondness – and he certainly gave them just what they ordered. He raised you up, smoothed out your face and spread your legs, making the women and boys go weak at the knees, the mothers sob and the men push out their chests and cocks. Christ but you must be tired.

I can't even look at you without my throat starting to ache with un-cried tears.

So here's an idea. Take a break. Read this – read it twice if you can be bothered – and then screw it up, toss it aside and come down. And I beseech you, don't do it at some magical, mythical, dream-sequence midnight; do it in the rush hour. Do it when the place is packed. Do it when nobody can believe their eyes. Clamber down when whistles are blowing and the hard-working dead-hearts are swarming off their trains, desperate for home and a drink or two; leave them screaming and slack-jawed and shitting in your wake, uselessly clicking shots on their phones as you trail wet bronze across Platform One, slouching monstrously towards the tube to dismay them down there too. Let people gibber that the dead are roaming, that they're looking for someone to shaft. Let word spread of three new sensations: Horror, Fear and Shame.

Think that might achieve something ?

You never know.

Sleep well.
Neil

———————————

Neil Bartlett
Brighton, Writer

My letter is dedicated to Fred Bartlett, my paternal grandfather.

My dear son

You are not really my son as I am French and you are
British, but you could be. Even if you were French, German,
you could be because you have in common with them all
the sufferings which have been imposed on you – that is
why I have decided to write to you: like fleas, rats, the
terrible smell of rotten flesh, nothing will have been spared
to make your life a hell. I think of you my dear son, I am
warm and you are cold, it rains on your neck and I can see
you tremble. And you are scared, I know it, and you are
supposed to be ashamed of it. Don't be, my son, you are
only human after all.

They forced you to hate your brothers, to kill them …
'Depuis six mille ans la guerre/Plaît aux peuples querelleurs/
Et Dieu perd son temps à faire/Les étoiles et les fleurs.' These
are words from Victor Hugo.

I find it painful to think that all those young lives, the
future of so many nations, should be sacrificed to the glory
of so few … and that you could be part of this so long
slaughter.

But, my son, apart from wellbeing, happiness is made of
short moments. Try to find them around you, in your very
limited corner: nature, flowers, friendship, sharing,
supporting one another …

Meanwhile, I will share with you what is left to me: hope,
without which life is not worth living. Hope for a better

future, when men can understand that it is better to sit at a table and talk when they feel insulted or hurt.

My son, keep, in your heart, the respect and compassion for your brothers of all nationalities, they suffer as much as you and didn't want to be forced to kill. May you feel warmed by my affection.

Yours,
Isabelle Schloesing

———————

Isabelle Schloesing
66, Southampton, French

To Papa from us all

I put on my big thinking cap – as you are done to call it – what to write and as you know we were never two for much scribeing since school days.

I sat with the holy terrors and us trying to think up what to say to Papa – words you could carry with you and I supposed it was those things – canny observations of yours that I was of a mind I would place down on paper for you in the way of remembering home here.

The yellow charlock and the shouts of the children from the river in summer, shouts what disappear – not in the wind, but like you one day pointed out to me – just when the boys have all gripped their noses together and gone feet first into Grimmers fish pool.

And there is that smelly byre of Old Halston you make us all quick step past come Sundays and there is the tips of them weeping willow fronds dragging in the river up toward Oughtibridge. Like idle fingers was what you once said.

Me and the children are sat in the back room with the blue tablecloth on and was trying to recall things you have pointed out to us in this past year or two. Gosh – two years gone since we all went and moved up here ? ?

We are all praying when you are over there that with these things you'll be minded to think on back home and us here and gain some goodness from such thoughts. On the bad days. Just think of them calls from the river and these yellowed up fields all about us – leasting that time of year ha ha. And we dont want you thinking just of whiskered Old Hastons smelly byre when your minded of home here ha ha.

Lucy is ripe with complaints having to only write on a messy slate up at the schoolhouse so I have promised her to write a few words here with proper pen on the good paper so.

Daddy
All me and my dolls want you back very soon if you
please
love you
Lucy

And Louis wants his say right here too

Dada today I saw a cat Louis x x

So there you have it husband. Carry this letter with you and
bring it and yourself both back to us.

Your loving wife always and Louis and Lucy.

[Note: Returned with other chattels by Ministry.]

_____

Alan Warner
Writer

Dear unknown soldier, I am the unknown great-grandson of the man you killed.

You were chosen for a raiding party. There were ten of you in all. You were a big man, strong arms and a farmer's grip. So you know why you were chosen. 'In case things get sticky', that's what the officer said. He'd seen you throw sandbags like they were nothing. He knew that if it came to the bayonet, the cudgel, the shovel or the fists, you'd be a good man to have on that raid.

In the end, you needed none of those. Your party found a way through the wire and surprised the German trench. Two men were taken, privates from Düsseldorf, both. But then there was movement in a dugout. Men's voices, the sound of boots on wood, rifles being shouldered. So you threw in a couple of Mills bombs. And then you and your party were gone, through the wire and into no-man's-land, a Maxim gun searching its shell holes. Behind you, in that dugout my great-grandfather was dying, a broken piece of wood through his throat and both his hands blown off at the wrist. By the time you reached your own trench, he was gone.

And so was I. Because of those Mills bombs he never returned from France. He never arrived home and went back to his job on the tourist boats on the Mosel river. So one summer's day he never saw my great-grandmother stepping out of a rowing boat. He never approached her to offer her his hand. They never made love a few weeks later. And so they never had a son who would have had a daughter of his own, who in turn would have given birth to me. Instead, because of you, we are all never.

A month after that raid your regiment were in the line again. An attack was ordered. Halfway across no-man's-land a shell landed at your feet. And then your children became never too. They found bits of you, but your name was lost. You were known but unknown. And I am sorry for that, I really am. I am sorry for it all. That you had to be a killer, and then had to be a killed. And despite what men did to each other in that war, and what they still do to each other now, I am sorry too, that I never got a chance to be. Life, for those lucky enough to live it, looks rather wonderful. I should have liked to taste its air, see its colours and know its love. I should have liked to have been known, not unknown. But instead I am never, along with the millions of other nevers born on those fields in France. Millions, who like me, are sorry. Sorry for it all.

———————————

Owen Sheers
Writer

Hello dear friend

Well I'm back to see you after 42 years. Forgive me, I'm the daughter of Ernie Leeson. He would insist each time we visited London that we would stand & look at you on platform 1 at Paddington after coming off the Welsh train.

Ernie, my dad, would explain who you were & what was so special about you. He told me about the Great War, how you could have fallen, how much you missed out on life. You watched over my dad when he waited in the Second World War for that train which would take him home, somewhere where you could not go. He would with his mates lean on you, sit by you or fall asleep around you in that war when London was bombed & blazed. You were his anchor in blind terror, when he tried to be brave in front of his mates. This I thank you that you helped my dad. Did you have an anchor, something that would not fail you, for you were this steely man for my dad.

My dad asked me who did I think your letter was from, back home I said, yes I know that, but who wrote his letter you looked so pleased to have. His mam I said. Was the letter from your mam? Did she tell you she was so proud of you, you need to keep yourself safe, say your prayers, don't drink too much, did you get the socks & scarf she knitted, Aunt Ethel has baked a cake for you & the lads. Me & your dad say our prayers every night that the Lord keeps you safe. You see I knew every word of that letter as that is what my mam & dad would have wrote to me.

And from me & my family our lives are so much richer because you stood up for freedom. Look at our world from the 100 years void, we have health care, pensions, education, laws which are becoming fairer for all, & so much more.

Thank you so much.

Lorraine Watkins née Leeson.

———————————

Lorraine Watkins
61, Newport, Post Office, Daughter

I have known this Statue all my life. My father who was in the 2nd WW used this statue as a meeting point, rest and sleeping place. I wanted the whole nation to know this tale. I dedicated this to my father Ernie Leeson who died in 1972 of his war wounds. He was a gentleman who believed in this country and never wanted to leave its shores again.

Nationalism is a curse. Empire is a curse. War, well, war is the curse that follows from these things with a rancid certainty. These abominations are still ongoing, and with each jump in technology and new generational façade of civility, they get subtly, and yet not so subtly, that much worse. You fought in what was trumpeted as 'the war to end them all'; such was the mindless barbarity, the pointless, inept cruelty of it. The same pigs, or their (more or less direct) descendants rather, are using the obscenity that was your death, and the deaths of millions like you, to stir up some misguided sense of 'national' solidarity among the poor, who they would send to suffer the same, a thousand times over if needed, to swell their coffers and their egos.

I'd like to think that perhaps you would agree. That these people use the blood of working-class kids to expand their deranged interests, their small, grasping lusts for wealth and control. But you're dead, and your voice cannot be heard. What can now be heard quite shrilly is the insincere sanctimony of scum like Cameron and Gove, claiming that while you might have had your misgivings, there in the mud, blood and excrement, watching your friends being marched into hails of bullets and shrapnel, that that war for oil, empire and ruling-class prestige that you were forced to die in, was to 'make the world a better place', rather than to satisfy the blood-drenched lunacy of their political forebears.

They invoke your name and speak of peace, and a desire to end war, while they sell tanks, planes and guns; the sort of terror that would stagger even you, to some of the most evil and barbarous despots alive today. Whether or not you would be outraged by their evil is conjecture, but I know too well that I am. They will use this centenary as a celebration, a carnival of vomitous jingoism. You have my sympathy that much more so.

Anonymous
Glasgow

The British state promotes a culture of militarism where it is viewed as heroic to go overseas and do murder for money. They are going to use the centenary, to this end, as a propaganda drive.

I don't know how to start this letter.

I feel like I should write Dear – because I want to be courteous, kind, respectful. But Dear Unknown Soldier feels like defeat before I have begun. If I name you, I will be imagining you into life, and you will no longer be unknown, not in quite the same way. Yet if I name you for someone who lived, then this becomes their story, and if I leave you Unknown, then this letter will be about me.

You have already received a lot of letters about people's own wars, and the wars of the people they love. There are many ways to fight a war and people need to tell their stories, and to see how they flow back into yours. Do you notice the trains, and the years, coming and going? Whatever we look at has the stain of your war.

For me – I want you to stay both unknown and known. You are someone I do not know, and cannot, but perhaps a family somewhere can still name you. How long will that last?

In our village is a war memorial, a mossy stone crucifix with an amphitheatre of names behind. They are the names of men from your war and the one that came after it, that you couldn't prevent. They are the names of those who didn't return. Not a lot of names, it was a small place then. And many are repeated: brother and brother, father and son, cousin and cousin.

Memorials are everywhere now, we barely notice them while they proclaim: lest we forget. I used your station for years before I noticed you. But a name is different. I cannot walk past the village memorial without stopping. Reading. Remembering a man I never met. A name is folded into history. It cannot be a symbol. It may be forgotten, but it cannot be changed and it cannot be used. It is. It was. It may be.

As I write this, men, women, and children are being killed half the world away and conflicts bubble across the globe. Most of the dead are not soldiers, most not even fighters. I cannot imagine what you would feel about these ongoing wars. But perhaps we can learn from you. An unknown soldier, like an unknown civilian, is only an unknown victim. And the first thing we do for a victim is to name him. It is instinctive. We know. Where there is a name, there is power, there is value, there is meaning, there is story.

When we name someone we recognise their wholeness and their humanness, a God-given identity. If we can do this with our friends, then perhaps we can begin to extend the same grace to our enemies? If we are ever to conquer war, and to make good on your sacrifice, then surely this is the place from which we must start?

Dear Unknown Soldier – what is your name?

With thanks,
Alexandra Carey

Alexandra Carey
27, Faversham, University of Kent, Writer

For my Great-Grandpa, who fought in the war that came later. This is inspired by the hope of peace, that there will not always be yet another war. For the courage to choose peace.

What made you go?
Did you go with friends or on your own?
What is the last thing you saw when you left home?
When you arrived in France, what did you notice first?

What do you fear most?
What sounds hurt you?
What food do you long for?
Have you had any moments of happiness since you left?
What were they?
What was the first death you saw?
What is the hour you most hate?
What part of the day is best?

Do you think often of home?
What do you miss?
What will be the first thing you'll want to do when you
    come home?
What do you like best about England?

Would you do it again?
What would you say to those who come after you?

How would you like to be remembered?
What didn't we understand?
What questions should we ask?

What is your name?
What is your name?
What is your name?

————————

Timberlake Wertenbaker
London, Playwright

Dear Papa

I know you will always be with me. You'll always want to play hide and seek with me, but I can't find you this time.

Am I not going to see you again when I hold my teddy bear and wait for a goodnight kiss? Am I not going to see you again running by the old cracking wooden table preparing breakfast for me and Mama? Am I?

Are you going to disappear in the dust that has been blown up by those iron bombs for ever?

I can always see your firm eyes flashing in my dream; I can also hear your steps when I looked outside. So I'm not afraid. I have a feeling that we are going to be puzzled in this war, parted for ever.

But Papa, you are not unknown – No matter what happened, you are always my dearest Papa. I will remember you. Mama will tell your story to that 90-year-old granny living next door.

See, I still remember you gave my mom warm coffee in a pretty china cup in a cold night!

That's why today when she accidently broke that cup,
She cried.
I picked the pieces up.
I hold them tightly until my fingers start to bleed.

———————

Anonymous
13, Croydon, Royal Russell School, Student

My teacher inspired me to write the homework. I would like to show that to all my friends.

Dear Leonard –

I want to call you by that name after Captain Leonard de Lona Christopher of the 40th Pathans who died at Ypres on 26 April 1915. The truth is, I've been calling you by that name since well before I thought to write this letter. You see, I pass by your statue quite often, and in the last few years while I've been reading about the Indian soldiers who served in WWI (500,000 of them) it's often struck me that while you are the Unknown Soldier there are some things about you that are known – which is to say, I know you aren't one of those Indian soldiers who are the first men my thoughts and heart move towards when I think of that terrible war you all fought.

But I don't want to stand in front of you, with everything you represent of loss, and think of the politics of Empire and race. There is a time and place for that, but you speak to a different impulse within me. And so, I've named you for Leonard de Lona Christopher even though, unlike you, he never fought in the trenches. He died on his first day of battle at Ypres on 26 April 1915. His regiment of Indian soldiers and British officers – the 40th Pathans – was in the first line of attack that had to cross over 1,000 metres of open ground to try and reach the German trenches. He died 'under fearful fire of machine guns and shells both front and flank'. In his dying moments, one of the Indian soldiers under his command loosened his belt. 'Mehrbani,' Captain Christopher said, in Urdu, meaning 'Thank you' or more specifically 'You've shown me a kindness'. And then he died.

When the vast brutal awful unnecessariness of the First World War is too much to hold in my head, this is what I think of: an Indian soldier stops in the middle of an open field with gunfire coming at him from every side to kneel beside a fallen man; he knows he can't stop the blood or heal the wounds, but equally he can't let this man die without making some gesture of comfort towards him. So he does all that is possible: he loosens the man's belt to allow him to breathe a little easier while breath remains. And the English officer, recognising the gesture, tells the soldier in his own language that his kindness has been recognised and appreciated.

I don't know the name of the Indian soldier. I hope he returned home.

Yours,
Kamila

Kamila Shamsie
London, Writer

Inchicore
Dublin
May 11th 1916.

My dear Seán,
              You will notice I have stuck two Post stamps
on the envelope to double the chance of you getting this
letter.
        This is because the General Post Office in Sackville St
was destroyed in the fighting over Easter. Most of the
centre of Dublin is gone.
        The authorities have over-reacted badly to the trouble
and have executed the Sinn Fein leaders including that
nice man Patrick Pearse with the funny eye who did the
rhymes. People are VERY angry here.
        With all this going on why don't you ask your
sergeant nicely to be moved back here where your local
knowledge would come in handy?
        You could also help control your wee brother Michael
who hasn't been the same since running messages for
that strange man De Valera at Boland's Mill during
the fighting.
        There is talk of a big push soon, maybe before you
get back, and you may be alongside Orangemen from
up north. Who would have imagined it — the
Dublin Fusiliers next that crowd, the 36th Division I
think they are?

Michael Gilmore
71, Bideford, Retired

They are good boys all the same, your cousin Aggie in Belfast worships her Sammy. You have probably run into him in France.

The good work you did in Turkey last year for that silly ass Mr Churchill may get you back here sooner — especially if you ask nicely.

We all hope to see you soon — keep away from those French lassies and remember your beads.

Sincerely,
Mammy.

My inspiration was the poem 'An Irish Airman Foresees His Death' by W. B. Yeats – 'Those that I fight I do not hate, those that I guard I do not love.' Dedicated to the large number of Irish troops who fought with a dilemma in 1914–1918.

Letter to my missing son

I see you walking boldly into the early morning sun, head held high, long easy strides, a half smile on your face, looking towards the horizon.

With hope and an open heart you set out to save the world.

And then you disappeared …

Where did you walk to my beloved son?

The sun rises every day, and still you are missing.

A trap had been perfectly set.

The loss is overwhelming, but I will never give up. Though my eyes grow dimmed with the tears shed, I will walk every path until I can no longer walk.

Oftentimes, in a crowd, my heart quickens. I catch a glimpse of a shadow, the turn of a head, the sound of a long-lost voice, of the music you played.

I thought I might die of grief 'you think you cannot keep breathing … and so that you may do it, God takes out your heart of flesh, and gives you a heart of stone.'

The door is wide open, you are a brave bold son, it is over, walk home.

Your ever-loving
Mum

———————————

Anonymous
66, Edinburgh, Grandmother

To all missing sons.

It is quiet in my pocket of London this afternoon dear soldier, a warm sultry summer's day, just as it might have been 100 years ago, the day before you signed up.

I am listening to the radio and thinking about how much more I know about you than I did a few short weeks ago.

All the different languages and nationalities you embody. The food you ate and yearned for. The farms and factories and families you left behind, and those who keep your memory alive even now. The reasons you joined up: adventure, duty, obligation, a belief in doing what you thought was right. The squalor and the fear, the lies, and the endless toll of death. How in the midst of blood and brutality there were still moments of beauty and resistance, camaraderie and kindness.

I am listening to the radio. It is 4 August 2014.

'This slaughter, this killing, must end,' says our Prime Minister.

Does it sound familiar, dear soldier?

Did you expect more from us?

———————————

Anna Vinegrad
London

To Gussie Vinn, who came home from the war and changed his name.

Tooting letter to the unknown soldier

Light of the moon. Star singing for the bird.
On lanes and land larks rise, witness all.
Beyond dark-water, beer-bottles, concerns.
Comfort taken in the cold awakes the scent of bitter herb
while you censor letters.
Lie down – the linnet calls.

Random who escapes and what remains untouched
by God's intervention. Yes – so have I heard.
And do in part believe. Heels hammer beat and home
on feet unsteady, towards the forest's burning fall.
Shells burst the invisible –
glory to the blackbird.

This morning chill hurts my skin. Delights my mind.
Sleeping awake in spring snow. Count and record
men – equal all: though some consigned to trucks.
All that is loved and daily left behind.
Polaris, singular, shines.
Don't know why – I could have cried.

───────────────

Cathy Galvin
54, London, Writer

*This letter-poem is dedicated to the poet Edward Thomas who
died when a shell burst near to him in the Great War and
sucked the oxygen from his body, destroying him without
leaving a mark. He lived near where I live in South-West
London for a large part of his life. In the quiet of his
extraordinary poetry and the few diary entries he made in his
war diary, we see a soul looking beyond the horror, listening*

for bird call. This sensibility was not sentimental. This letter is for him. One of Thomas's jobs as an officer was to censor letters. It's for my lover too who first showed me the statue which has inspired this wonderful project.

Still waiting for your train, my friend? I'll wait with you. You look like you could use the company. You look … tired. Please don't think me rude for saying it. I'm tired too. I've seldom been so tired. We've been working hard, you and I. Side-by-side, brothers-in-arms. You seem unsure, friend. You can't quite place me. Don't worry, it'll come to you. You've known me in passing. Now let's rest a while. Let's hold our tongues. I can hear birds, can you? Little birds in the sky. They said the birds stopped singing, silly fools. The birds never stopped; you just stopped listening. Let's be quiet a while. Perhaps a smoke. A nice scarf you've got there, friend. From your mother, from your sweetheart? I'd offer you a cigarette but I don't believe we've time. Here it comes. The Last Train. You wait and wait, and still it's sooner than you hoped. I'll leave you go, friend. No, no. I'm not catching this myself. I'll close the doors, and blow the whistle. All aboard. All aboard.

Nathan Filer
Writer

Dear Dad,

I hope you come back alive instead of dead because I would have no chance surviving in the front line but, I know you would, because of your bravery and strength. If you do happen to die I will remember you with all my heart and I will tells everyone how brave you were. Please can you try not to die so the fun can go on. So just remember, I am Supporting you, even when you're in a tough situation.

When you come home (if you survive) there will be a huge suprise! And I promise it will be fun. Even though you're in the front line I know you can do it. The only three things I ask are: number one: send me a letter every week, number two: try not to die and number 3: win the war!!! I know, I know I have been putting you off but heres the fun part. If you come back mum is going to take you to a famous night club and wants to kiss you! auw right?

Love your son Ryan
P.S don't tell mum about the night club

Ryan Cahalan
9, London

Na biodh feagal ort. Cha mhair an t-sàmhchair seo fada.

Cluinnidh tu an t-àit' ud a' gairm ort. Fhathast an sin a' feitheamh, an fheadhainn a bhios a' faighneachd gu sìorraidh: "Càit' an do lorg e am bàs? Cà' bheil na cnàmhan geal aige nan laighe?"

Èirichidh tu, a ghaisgich dhàn, is fàgaidh tu do ghunna 's do bhleigleid air do chùlaibh. Lorgaidh tu rathad aithnichte agus leanaidh tu na guthan aca air ais gu àrainneachd d' òige. Gu talamh dubh do dhaoine.

Ach gus an tig an latha sin – a' mhic stròdhail, a' ghille chaillte – fuirich thus' nad chadal. Bidh tu feumach air fois airson a' chuairt fhada dhachaigh.

Don't be afraid. This silence will not last long.

You will hear that place call you up. Still there waiting, those that forever ask: 'Where did he find death? Where do his white bones lie?'

You will rise, brave fighter, and you will leave your gun and bayonet behind. You will find a familiar road and you will follow their voices back to the landscape of your youth. To the black earth of your people.

But until that day comes – prodigal son, lost boy – stay sleeping. You will need to rest for the long walk home.

———————————

Catriona Lexy Campbell
Writer, Scotland

Afterword

Neil Bartlett and Kate Pullinger's *Letter to an Unknown Soldier* is an inspired project that has captured the imagination of people across the UK and beyond. Reading the huge number of letters that poured in over the six weeks from 28 June to 4 August 2014, one of the most striking features is the sheer diversity of stories, questions, perspectives and motivations of the letter-writers, all contributing to a rich portrait of how people in the UK feel about the First World War, one hundred years on.

We can look up the statistics from the First World War – the lists and numbers of those killed, wounded, the battles, the villages and towns destroyed. We can read history books that tell us part of the story, but artists can unlock emotion, empathy and creativity; can help us to understand.

Our perceptions of the First World War have been shaped to a great extent by the artists of the time – the poets, writers, painters, sculptors, composers, photographers and film-makers, many of whom served, and who reflected on the war and its effects on individuals and society. Their art had a profound and lasting impact. One hundred years later, 14-18 NOW is inviting contemporary artists from the UK and around the world to explore the resonance of the First World War today. *Letter to an Unknown Soldier* was among the very first of these commissions. This anthology and the digital archive of all 21,439 letters will together ensure that the letters reach an even wider readership.

We are grateful to HarperCollins for publishing the book, Free Word for producing the project, to the Imperial War Museum and British Library, to our funders Arts Council England, Heritage Lottery Fund and DCMS, and most of all to Neil Bartlett and Kate Pullinger, for conceiving and championing this project, and to all the letter-writers who have together created a profoundly moving contribution to the Centenary.

Jenny Waldman
Director,
14-18 NOW – WW1 Centenary Art Commissions

List of Contributors

1914 Sikhs
Dom Agius
Yasmin Alibhai-Brown
David Almond
Muhammad Hassan Anwar
Chelsea Asher
Neil Bartlett
Benjamin Elliott Barton
June Bilton
Alistair Boucher
Bette Bourne
Matthew Burford
Neil Burke
Ryan Cahalan
David Cameron
Catriona Lexy Campbell
Alexandra Carey
Andrew Carter
Lee Child
Jason Chua
Caryl Churchill
Pam Clatworthy
Stephen Cleator
Jo Clifford

Sophie Collard
Shane Cook
Amanda Craig
Archie Darroch
Martin Daws
Jill Dawson
Emily Duke
Geoff Dyer
Elizabeth
Inua Ellams
Ellie
Bernardine Evaristo
Nathan Filer
Freya Finch Atter
Stuart Fink
Aminatta Forna
Roseby Franklin
Dawn French
Thomas Frith
Stephen Fry
Cathy Galvin
Vanessa Gebbie
Michael Gilmore
Dennis Gimes

Diana Goldsworthy
Sam Greening
Mark Haddon
Sheila Hancock
Rebecca Harris
Demelza Hauser
Gill Hawkes
Kirsty Rachael Heyam
Vikki Heywood
Alyssa Hollingsworth
Richard Ireson
Sharon J.
Roger Jarman
Deborah Jones
Graham Hugh Jones
Owen Jones
A. L. Kennedy
S. Khan
Azmeena Ladha
Mateo Lara
Bryony Lavery
Thomas Steven Burnham
   Lee
Deborah Levy
Tricia Lloyd Waller
Siobhan Logan
Amanda Loutfi
Caroline Lucas
Joanna Lumley
Sandra Lyon
Margaret MacMillan
Andy McNab
Hollie McNish
Angela McSherry

Doreen McSherry
Kathy Miles
Ed Miliband
Mary Moran
Donald W. Morrison
Andrew Motion
Nabil M. Mustapha
Daljit Nagra
Bernadette Oldfield
John Owen
Sue Oxley
Roxanne Peak-Payne
Stephen Pelton
Denise Perrin
Kate Pullinger
Oska Read
Barry Rees
Georgina Rees
Gwynyth Joy Revitt
Anna Sandham
Isabelle Schloesing
Gareth Scourfield
Sean
Kamila Shamsie
Owen Sheers
Shelagh
Colin Shields
Alex Sinclair
Jackie Snowman
Sarah Spain
Sean Spain
Nathalie Stocks
Dr Manish Tayal
Patricia Taylor

Roberta Taylor
Lisa Turrell
Anna Vinegrad
Rob Walton
Alan Warner
Lorraine Watkins
Louise Welsh
Timberlake Wertenbaker

Jacqueline Westrop
Patrick Widdess
Dafydd Williams
Clare Marci Wilson
Benjamin Zephaniah

And 10 anonymous
contributors

Acknowledgements

Kate Pullinger and Neil Bartlett would like to thank the
following people for their help with *Letter to an Unknown
Soldier* and this book: 14-18 NOW WW1 Centenary Art
Commissions, Dom Agius, Arts Council England, Chelsea
Asher, Bath Spa University, BBC, Bolton & Quinn, Laura
Bradshaw, British Library, Effect, Empire Café, Free Word,
Daniel Goddard, Sarah Goodfellow, Alessandra Grignaschi,
Kathleen Hamilton, Ruth Harrison, Lisa Heledd Jones,
Heritage Lottery Fund, Alyssa Hollingsworth, Mab Jones,
Lily Kerfoot, Ruth Mackenzie, Angela McSherry, Rosie
Maynard, Liz Milner, Network Rail and team at Paddington
Station, Tim Parry, Roxanne Peak-Payne, Allic Rennie, Sean
Spain, Polly Steele, Katie Stuart, The Cogency, The Unloved,
The Verbal Arts Centre, Rosie Tobutt, Anna Vinegrad,
Jenny Waldman, Murray Wason, Dave Watson, Nicky
Webb, William Collins, Timothy X Atack, You, Me +
Everyone and all the 21,439 individuals who contributed
to the *Letter to an Unknown Soldier* project in the summer
of 2014.